Cultivating Democratic Literacy Through the Arts

A volume in
Advances in Teacher Education
Diane Yendol-Hoppey and David T. Hoppey, *Series Editors*

Advances in Teacher Education

Diane Yendol-Hoppey and David T. Hoppey, *Series Editors*

Professional Learning Journeys of Teacher Educators (2024)
    Brandon M. Butler and Jason K. Ritter

Pathways Into Teacher Education: Profiles of Emerging Teacher Educator Development (2023)
    Brandon M. Butler, Alexander Cuenca, and Jason K. Ritter

Exemplary Clinical Models of Teacher Education (2023)
    Sara R. Helfrich and Sara L. Hartman

(Re)Designing Programs: A Vision for Equity-Centered, Clinically Based Teacher Preparation (2021)
    Jennifer Jacobs and Rebecca West Burns

Collaboration, Narrative, and Inquiry That Honor the Complexity of Teacher Education (2020)
    Amy Johnson Lachuk, Karen Rut Gísladóttir, and Tricia DeGraff

Preparing the Next Generation of Teacher Educators for Clinical Practice (2019)
    Diane Yendol-Hoppey, Nancy Fichtman Dana, and David T. Hoppey

Outcomes of High-Quality Clinical Practice in Teacher Education (2018)
    Diane Yendol-Hoppey and David T. Hoppey

Working Together: Enhancing Urban Educator Quality Through School-University Partnerships (2017)
    Diane Yendol-Hoppey, Deborah Shanley, Darby C. Delane, and David T. Hoppey

Dispositions in Teacher Education (2007)
    Mary Diez and James Raths

What Counts as Knowledge in Teacher Education (Volume 5) (2005)
    James Raths

Teacher Beliefs and Classroom Performance: The Impact of Teacher Education (2003)
    James Raths and Amy C. McAninch

Cultivating Democratic Literacy Through the Arts

Guiding Preservice Teachers Towards Innovative Learning Spaces in ELA Classrooms

edited by

Pamela Hartman
Ball State University

Jeff Spanke
Ball State University

INFORMATION AGE PUBLISHING, INC.
Charlotte, NC • www.infoagepub.com

Library of Congress Cataloging-in-Publication Data

A CIP record for this book is available from the Library of Congress
http://www.loc.gov

ISBN: 979-8-88730-571-4 (Paperback)
       979-8-88730-572-1 (Hardcover)
       979-8-88730-573-8 (E-Book)

Copyright © 2024 Information Age Publishing Inc.

All rights reserved. No part of this publication may be reproduced, stored in a retrieval system, or transmitted, in any form or by any means, electronic, mechanical, photocopying, microfilming, recording or otherwise, without written permission from the publisher.

Printed in the United States of America

CONTENTS

Introduction: "Look Them in the Eye So That They Know You're Human" vii

1 Act Like a Teacher: Shaping Future Educators Through Drama-Based Pre-Service Pedagogy 1
Jaydene Elvin and Andy Waldron

2 Building a Photographic Teaching Philosophy: ELA Preservice Teachers' Journey to See the Unseen 17
Pamela Hartman and Dani Tinkel

3 Tapestries of Teaching: Flagging Philosophies of Education in Preservice Curriculum 37
Jeff Spanke

4 Using Visual Storytelling to Support Democratic Approaches to Literacy Instruction 55
Wendy R. Williams

5 Ideas Unscrapped: Repurposing Metal to Support Identity Building in Writing 71
S. Rebecca Leigh

6 Wood and Words: Woodworking as an Analogue for Teaching and Writing 87
Lee Douma

7 Using Book Study to Support Multigenre Ensembles in
  Teacher Preparation.. 99
  Pauline Schmidt and Matthew Kruger-Ross

8 Finding a Light in the *Night*: An Opportunity for the Arts
  to Illuminate the Way... 115
  Timothy J. Duggan and Joshua Smith

INTRODUCTION

"Look Them in the Eye So That They Know You're Human"

On Wednesday, June 3rd, 2020, eight days after the killing of George Floyd, a group of protesters spilled into the typically sparse streets of Whitefish, Montana. Like so many thousands more around the United States during that first COVID summer, these anguished citizens wore masks, carried signs, and chanted the names of Black men and women who lost their lives in police custody, all while demanding that Black lives do matter and that racism kills.

Amidst the otherwise peaceful throngs of resistance and fatigue, a 51-year-old White man named Jay Snowden started berating people in the Montana crowd, hurling profanities and clenching his fists in threatening gestures of violence. Eventually, Snowden aimed his verbal assault at Samantha Francine, a Black Whitefish woman who clutched a modest sign containing the words: *Say Their Names*. The ensuing three-minute tirade was recorded by local journalist Grace Jensen, and the video immediately went viral. Within days, the jarring clip had circulated the globe, drawing international attention to the stark division that was plaguing even the most remote of American towns.

But it was a still image from the viral phenomenon—a single black and white frame from Jensen's video—that garnered nearly as much fascination as the source material itself. Roughly fifteen seconds into the exchange

---

Cultivating Democratic Literacy Through the Arts, pages vii–xvii
Copyright © 2024 by Information Age Publishing
www.infoagepub.com
All rights of reproduction in any form reserved.

between Snowden and Francine, the recording captures the shorter, masked Francine lifting her sunglasses to look her unmasked, White male attacker in the eye.

The image shows an enraged Snowden, his back to the camera, fists clenched and primed, mouth agape, the veins in his bent arms nearly popping through his skin. He stands, feet shoulder-width apart, with an arched, flexed back, looking down on the woman just inches below.

Francine, still wearing her mask and holding her sign, had lifted her sunglasses, her shoulders squared in a defiant display of confidence and strength. She shows no fear. No cowardice. We see the whites of her eyes, the light from the sun having captured them from behind the shadow cast by Snowden's camouflage baseball cap. We see other people in the image: one blurry figure slightly behind Francine and another motioning to something in the distance, his face cut off by the frame. But our focus remains on Snowden and Francine. They have claimed the foreground, their moment having become our world. Or maybe vice versa. Without any context or additional information, we do not know the people in this picture; yet at the same time, the woman's sign compels us to simply, yet in the face of violent opposition, say their names, this plea offering a caption, of sorts, for the scene.

Less than a month after the altercation between Snowden and Francine, a columnist for *Montana Woman Magazine* named Megan Crawford authored an article entitled "Samantha Francine: You Belong Here." In her piece, Crawford ruminates on the image taken from Jensen's original video, juxtaposing the artifact against the racial turmoil that reached a national boiling point in the summer of 2020. In the article, Crawford extends upon the profundity of Francine lifting her sunglasses to confront Snowden. "No matter who the threat is," Crawford wrote, "no matter what the threat is, you look them in the eye so that they know you're human" (Crawford, 2020).

Indeed, one could argue that without Francine's eyes, the picture never would have gathered enough steam to make it out of Whitefish. Her eyes give the image-as-text a unique context and backstory that warrant further inquiry, consideration, and discernment. They offer a sequence, of sorts: a narrative structure that both reflects and rejects the external world that spawned it. They turn the picture into art.

Her eyes invite us to ponder the sign and its message; Snowden and his back; the veins and the masks and everything that is happening around them. The sunglasses, now without function. Her eyes prompt us to make meaning from the image, to give it a purpose, and to help us learn a little bit more about how we, as citizens looking on from afar, might negotiate our own roles in the world that those eyes see. Because, truly, when it comes to this image, hers is the only vision we have.

* * *

At the same time that Jensen's video was making its global waves—joining the endless wake of COVID memes, political poems, paintings, and posters; and other forms of protest art—we, the editors, decided that we wanted to make our own contribution to the wider conversation happening around us. Specifically, the events of the summer of 2020 reignited a latent passion in the two of us to explore the power of art, its saturation in our literacy culture, and how, just as we were witnessing throughout our country, it can empower our preservice English Language Arts (ELA) teachers. As English teachers, literacy instructors, and teacher educators we each appreciated the unique knowledge structures, dispositions, and skillsets needed to engage with these aesthetic cultural artifacts in productive, progressive ways. After all, it takes a certain kind of literacy to read a meme, and analyzing a poster, explicating a sculpture, or unpacking a piece of music demands a different cognitive process than making meaning of a manual or cookbook. Truly, there's a particular habit of mind (Eisner, 2002) involved in engaging with the world through an artistic lens; so much so that, oftentimes, the engagement itself can take on an aesthetic, arts-based means of its own, evolving the notion of "arts-based" from the *object* of our pursuits—art, as a thing to be studied—to the verb, the habit of mind, that characterizes the aesthetic means by which we study.

In other words, while much of the existing scholarship and arts-education focuses on studying art or using art as a pedagogical aid, this book strives to promote art almost as a verb in itself; the aesthetic means through/with which we engage with education holistically. Just as curriculum has its roots in the Latin verb "currere," meaning "to run," we propose in this book that art can function just as efficaciously in ELA preservice methods classes as a verb as it does as a noun. In this sense, as odd as it may sound, as preservice ELA teachers and English teacher educators, we don't just study art or make art. We, quite simply, art.

Along these lines, as we continued exploring the implications for art-as-process in ELA teacher education, we also recognized the profound intersections between aesthetic artifacts and the critical civic literacies they promote (DeVitis, 2011). For, truly, it is difficult to analyze Grace Jensen's photo of Samantha Francine and Jay Snowden without somehow employing a particular type of arts-based literacy that tethers the conversation in some way to notions of community, justice, or broader notions of citizenship or humanity.

And, of course, this is nothing new.

In a sense, art has always served as a vehicle to respond to, reject, revise, or at the very least reimagine the external contexts whence it came. When it comes to American landscape paintings, for example—those sweeping, bucolic tapestries of nineteenth century American pastoralism that typically adorn the walls of museum lobbies or politicians' offices—Miller (2009) argues that "the contemporary symbolism contained in these well-known works of [art] are a muted echo of the even fuller response they once provoked" (p. 85). More than simply hotel art or waiting room décor, in their day, American landscape paintings functioned as "exemplary vehicles for the transmission of republican behaviors and attitudes... and the connective tissue that might rebuild civic bonds" (Barrett, 2013, p. 26–27). In fact, early American cultural thinkers emphasized painting's capacity to "communicate the central attitudes necessary for [citizenship] and to temper those impulses believed to promote disorder" (p. 28). The early nineteenth century politician, Giulian Verplanck saw painting in particular as a viable mechanism to preserve public stability by bridging the gap between the individual citizen and the abstractions of political ideology.

In other words, what some may see as simply pretty mountains or romanticized renditions of America's infancy, blurred, perhaps, above a mantel in the background of a *Hallmark* Christmas movie, may, in reality, have originated as incendiary reactions towards the perils of Jacksonian Democracy (Miller, 1989). Just because these paintings (or their creators) may remain banished to the obscurities of our collective subconscious doesn't mean that their efficacy as poignant sources of astute social commentary and critical civic literacies has waned. These artists simply mixed pigments while Grace Jensen shoots film.

In this sense, American landscape paintings offer a reminder that all art may serve not only aesthetic but democratically progressive ends. Rogers, et al. (2015) argue that "we can view civic engagement in part through the perspective of resistance" (p. 112). Here again, we see staunch political resistance manifested through art not only in the landscape paintings of artists like Thomas Cole or other painters of the Hudson River School (Truetner and Wallach, 1994), but also in Grace Jensen's depiction of Samantha Francine's eyes. That we see them at all signifies her resistance to all that Jay Snowden personified that day in Whitefish, Montana.

Especially given the vitriol that now seems to characterize the summer of 2020, the various aesthetic artifacts that emerged during these months of crises both prompted and responded to various socio/cultural/political backlashes. Not only are the moments that inspired these artifacts contested, but the artifacts that precipitated from them are certainly not without dispute. Still, because these moments and artifacts compel us to consider the ways we interact with the world and, by extension, discern how we shape and are shaped by our environments, these artifacts also promoted the cultivation of critical civic literacy insofar as they demand that audiences "actively [question] assumptions about what it means to be a democratic citizen and even who counts as a citizen in our society" (Mayo, 2011, p. 424).

While Teitlebaum (2010) argues that "civic literacy means being well-versed in social and political knowledge, understandings, dispositions, and skills" (p. 309), Mayo (2011) notes that *critical* civic literacy can help develop citizens who are "particularly concerned with exposing and undoing systems of privilege and oppression in the hopes of attaining equity for all" (p. 424). If Samantha Francine's eyes did anything in Jensen's picture, it simultaneously reveals and dismantles the systems of privilege and oppression that the Jay Snowdens of the world perpetuate and enjoy. We cannot engage with the images and moments without doing so through the lens of critical civic literacy. The art begets the lens, which in turn, begets more art.

In serving activist ends, as well as aesthetic ones, art also embodies Hatt and Parkinson's (2011) contention that "critical civic literacy affords the opportunity to reassert the goal of democratic equality for public education. It is an essential step toward asking students and policy makers: education for whom and for what ends?" (p. 389). When anchored in a series of guiding questions, critical civic literacy echoes the promise of the "Philosophy for Children" movement that emerged in the 1970s, as well as the subsequent Community of Philosophical Inquiry (CPI) "method" that stemmed from this approach (Lipman, 2003:1976; Lipman, et al., 1980; Matthews, 2002: 1980: 1976). "To become a member of a community of inquiry," writes Sharp (1997), "is to commit to ongoing, self-conscious reconstruction of one's worldview as the inquiry proceeds" (p. 75). We argue that the same can be said of any act of literacy.

In order to engage in literacy, we must make constant decisions. Compose, then decompose. Weigh, measure, and assess. Delete, supplement, and constantly order. Literacy demands that we add and subtract, evolve and revise. In this sense, engaging with acts of literacy necessitates the same cognitive and intellectual processes as those demanded by acts of inquiry. Yet, as Sharp (1997) continues, when it comes to acts of literacy and inquiry, "aren't these the very activities that the painter engages in as she works on her canvas or the novelist engages as he develops his story?" (p. 76). The chapters in this book seek to highlight this intersection of critical civic literacy, communities of inquiry, and art.

Of course, also at this intersection is the role of education, particularly teacher education. Each of the chapters in this book speaks specifically to how arts-based instruction can infuse preservice ELA education, a field of study very much lacking in the current literature. As Giorza (2016) found, "the [community of philosophical inquiry], in combination with contemporary visual art analysis, [offers] a way of learning together through dialogue and reflection [and suggests] that the approach provides better access to the practice of academic argumentation than the more commonly used text-based approaches" (p. 178). Giorza (2016) further argues that marbling CPI with arts-based instruction "has the potential to generate deep and personally relevant learning" (p. 177) for preservice teachers. Indeed, in our work as colleagues and English teacher educators, we have found over the years that marbling the tenets of CPI and arts-based instruction can have profound impacts on the habits of mind and developing teacher disposition of our preservice candidates. As mentioned above, it was our combined history of arts-informed pedagogy that, when placed against a backdrop of the national climate circa 2020, inspired the creation of this book.

Nevertheless, despite positive contributions in the fields of CPI, arts-based instruction, and citizenship education as English teacher educators, we recognize that, while much has been written about these distinct curricular models over the last half century, very little of this work seems focused specifically on examining how these approaches might intersect at the teacher education level. Research has demonstrated the importance of art in education overall, but much of this work remains woefully limited, particularly at the secondary level. And while professional texts discuss activities that lend themselves to K–12 classrooms, there is little to no research regarding how to employ arts-based pedagogies in college-level methods classrooms in order for teacher candidates to gain hands-on experience and to create the habits of mind necessary for their own future arts-based instruction. In short, this book endeavors to shine light on a topic that is virtually non-existent in secondary ELA methods courses.

What could it look like to infuse ELA *methods* instruction with arts-based curriculum? What if that curriculum has its roots in democratic literacies, citizenship development, or the methods offered by the Community of Philosophical Inquiry model? What do those words even *mean*, anyway, and what place do they have in ELA teacher education? How might we prepare future teachers to incorporate arts-based democratic literacies or critical civic inquiries in their own classrooms? Terms like social justice and equity have (rightfully) made their way into the lexicons of ELA teacher education; but what do we mean when we say things like *critical civic literacies* or *democratic citizenship* in an ELA context? And again, what do these ideas have to do with art? We offer this book in the spirit of addressing these questions.

This is a book about teaching, for teachers and teacher educators. It is about the powerful role that art plays, not only throughout education, but specifically in secondary English Language Arts. More to the point, this book is about helping preservice teachers and teacher educators consider ways in which art can be used in secondary classrooms. We see this book being used in secondary ELA methods courses by educators who understand the values that lie at the intersection of critical civic literacy, inquiry, and art. This book is equal parts methodological and pedagogical, philosophical and conceptual. But mostly, it's grounded in the notion that as ELA teachers we, not only have the joy of teaching with and through art, but also derive joy in knowing that teaching, in itself, is an art.

We argue in this book that the same can be said not just for education on a broad, noninstitutional level, but more specifically on the level of ELA teacher education. As teachers of literacy and English Language Arts, we agree with Elliot Eisner's argument that "literacy itself cannot be limited to what the tongue can articulate but to what the mind can grasp. Thus, in this sense"—and as the chapters in this book highlight—"dance, music, and the visual arts are languages through which meaning and mind are promoted" (2003, p. 342). These chapters not only support Eisner's claims about the multifaceted and inherently aesthetic parameters of literacy, but extend upon them to promote communities of philosophical inquiry and democratic citizenship in ELA methods courses.

We also agree with Eisner when he says that "in a free democratic state, at least a part of the role of education is to help youngsters learn how to define their own purposes" (2005, p. 189). Yet while this process of self-actualization should, in part, be facilitated by artistic exploration and creation, we argue that it is also inextricably linked to notions of community, democracy, and citizenship; in other words, the definitions of the students' "own purposes" that Eisner lauds as byproduct of education only bear significance when existing within a free, democratic discursive space. Eisner's "youngsters" have always been citizens by another name, and the purposes they define for themselves should ideally serve not only their interests but also the interests of their greater world. "Such an orientation to knowledge," Eisner continues, "would reduce the tendency for students to regard the textbook as sacred and knowledge as fixed—not a bad outcome for a nation that prides itself on being a democracy" (2002, p. 103). We couldn't agree more.

Ultimately, this book endeavors to extend the notion of arts education to secondary, ELA preservice teacher education. Each of the following chapters focuses on a particular artistic tradition or modality and is composed by experts in the field of ELA instruction (?) who speak to how their respective artistic modes might be taken up in an ELA methods context. Given our emphasis on the conceptual and curricular ties between critical civic literacy, arts education, and democratic citizenship, we offer this book in the spirit of helping teacher educators and preservice teachers navigate these issues in their future classrooms. We hope that the philosophies and projects shared by these authors could serve as a springboard from which other stakeholders might begin cultivating their own habits of mind regarding art's role in teacher preparation.

THE BOOK THAT FOLLOWS:
THE CHAPTERS AND OUR CHARGE

Literacy, according to the National Council of Teachers of English, is more than the ability to read and write. "At its simplest, literacy is the way that we interact with the world around us, how we shape it and are shaped by it.

It is how we communicate with others via reading and writing, but also by speaking, listening, and creating." *Democratic*, or critical civic literacy, by extension, involves the degree to which our interaction with the world—our shaping both of and by it—derives from membership in various communities. It refers to how we engage with literacy *as citizens* within our worlds: citizens with rights and responsibilities, powers and privileges, and worlds full of structures and systems. Critical civic, or democratic, literacy, in this sense, involves the inquiry-based literacy practices by which citizens challenge these structures, seek equity, and promote democracy in their communities. For this book, we ground these terms and definitions in an aesthetic foundation, hoping to explore how art can be used in secondary ELA instruction to promote the type of critical literacy that democracies need.

In this book, we hear from teacher educators and researchers who investigate new arts-based instructional approaches to teach democratic literacy. Specifically, they research these approaches by implementing them into their own curriculum and instruction while teaching preservice courses. The models presented here are meant to increase preservice teachers' understanding of arts-based literacy instruction through experiential learning and to inspire them to implement and experiment with these pedagogies in their future ELA classrooms.

Since effective teaching requires the confidence and communicative skills to stand up in front of groups of people, as well as the flexibility to respond to the unexpected, Jaydene Elvin and Andy Waldron explore innovative, drama-based pedagogical approaches to achieve these goals. They use movement, voice, and improvisation techniques in teacher training to help pre-service and novice teachers develop essential skills. They also provide all teachers, including those teaching or intending to teach English Language Arts (ELA) and literacy, with strategies that they can use to improve their teaching skills and pedagogical approaches for the classroom.

Several of our authors consider how to implement visual arts in ELA teacher education courses to facilitate learning. Pamela Hartman and Dani Tinkel provide an example of how to use photography to encourage ELA teacher candidates to analyze photographic texts and to use their own photography to facilitate aesthetic and narrative thinking. Through this process, the students delve into their own beliefs and about teaching and learning and create visual representations of their philosophies of education.

Jeff Spanke's chapter reflects upon an assignment he created for his Introduction to English Education course that involved the creation of "Teaching Flags." Inspired by his work with international students, Jeff's "Flags Assignment" asked preservice teachers to create a series of artifacts that reflect their values, principles, and constitutions as future teachers. More so than a teaching philosophy, the flags served to position the students as citizens within the broader teaching community. Jeff discusses the origins of the Flags Assignment, its initial execution, and implications for fellow teacher educations and the teaching community as a whole.

Wendy Williams examines visual storytelling's potential for supporting democratic approaches to literacy learning. She first explores some of the ways that comics, graphic novels, and zines have been used in education and then looks at how visual storytelling was used in a university-level YA literature course. In doing so, she shares findings from a qualitative case study of three students in this course and discusses these findings' implications for teaching.

The next two chapters use art—etched art and woodworking—to generate metaphors for thinking about teaching and writing. Rebecca Leigh explores the author's former literacy teaching practices and how these practices have evolved over the years for the author through her teaching of aesthetic writing. Examples are framed by her work in a seven-day summer workshop with students, which includes painting metal with acid. The metal's transformation is used to support vivid and descriptive writing. Through her discussions with preservice teachers, she helps them interrogate their beliefs about writing by showing them examples of what students are capable of writing when the invitation involves artistic strategies and thinking. She also shares the shifts in her own thinking that were necessary to teach more effectively.

Lee Douma investigates numerous analogies drawn between the process of woodworking and the processes of teaching and writing. The various steps in this process—harvesting wood, splitting, cutting, sculpting, sanding, and finishing—are compared to the processes of choosing content for a lesson or text, structuring arguments and instruction, choosing evidence and pedagogical methods, examining potential objections, and other nuances of effective teaching and writing. These connections are made explicitly but with occasional nods toward the poetic elements of these endeavors.

Pauline Schmidt & Matthew Kruger-Ross describe the development and implementation of a course for preservice teachers (PSTs) that aims to cultivate democratic literacy through a series of multigenre assignments called "Book Study." The key method or approach to achieve this aim is driven by multimodal, multigenre, and arts-based pedagogies. They show how interdisciplinary groups of PSTs worked together to read, review, analyze, and study books that highlight democratic practices and literacies. They also provide specific strategies and activities that emerge from multimodal and arts-based pedagogies that are critical in developing democratic literacy.

Finally, Tim Duggan and Joshua Smith illustrate how English language arts teacher educators can encourage teacher candidates to bring their artistic knowledge and interests into their practice. This secondary education professor and a student teacher share their personal artistic journeys and describe how arts integration in a secondary ELA methods class (as well as other classes) led one teacher candidate to design an engaging student teaching unit on Elie Wiesel's Holocaust memoir, *Night*. The teacher candidate's own students were encouraged to create visual and musical responses to Wiesel's text as a way of understanding how to make a counterargument. The instructional unit is connected to current theory and scholarship on arts integration and includes both a teacher artistic model and student work samples, as well as analysis of student-generated artifacts.

We want our preservice teachers to have a deep understanding of their pedagogy. To do so, we want them to do more than simply *read about* critical theories and effective teaching strategies. We believe that they need hands-on experience learning through these artistic methods themselves. In this way, they will develop the habits of mind that they will need to effectively discuss, produce, and implement these kinds of artistic strategies to promote their students' literacy in positive, engaging, and democratic ways.

REFERENCES

Barrett, T. (2013). Thomas Cole, republican aesthetics, and the political jeremiad. *American Art, 27*(1), 24–49.
Crawford, M. (2020). Samantha Freeman: You belong here. *Montana Woman Magazine*.
DeVitis, J. L. (Ed.). (2011). *Critical civic literacy: A reader*. Peter Lang.
Eisner, E. W. (2005). *Reimagining schools: The selected works of Elliot Eisner*. Routledge.
Eisner, E. W. (2003). The arts and the creation of the mind. *Language Arts, 80*(5), 340–344.
Eisner, E. W. (2002). *The arts and the creation of mind*. Yale University Press.
Eisner, E. W. (1965). Curriculum ideas in a time of crisis. *Art Education, 18*(7), 7–12.
Eisner, E. W. (1958). What is art education for? *The High School Journal, 41*(6), 263–267.
Giorza, T. (2016). Thinking together through pictures: The community of philosophical inquiry and visual analysis as transformative pedagogy. *Perspectives in Education, 34*(1), 167–181.
Hatt, B., & Parkinson, P. (2011). Writing to read: Critical civic literacy at an alternative school. In J. L. DeVitis. (Ed.). *Critical civic literacy: A reader* (pp. 381–392). Peter Lang.
Lipman, M. (2003). *Thinking in education*. Cambridge University Press.
Lipmann, M., Sharp, A. M., & Oscanyan, F. S. (1980). *Philosophy in the classroom*. Temple University Press.
Lipman, M. (1976). Philosophy for children. *Metaphilosophy, 7*(1), 17–39.
Matthews, G. (1994). *Philosophy of childhood*. Harvard University Press.
Matthews, G. (1980). *Philosophy and the young child*. Harvard University Press.
Matthews, G. (1976). Philosophy and children's literature. *Metaphilosophy, 7*(1), 7–16.
Mayo, J. B. (2011). Social justice enacted: Critical civic engagement in the gay straight alliance. In J. L. DeVitis (Ed.). *Critical civic literacy: A reader* (pp. 419–430). Peter Lang.

Miller, A. (1989). Thomas Cole and Jacksonian America: The course of an empire as political allegory. *Prospects, 14*, 65–92.

NCTE Standing Committee on Global Citizenship National Council of Teachers of English. (2020). *Literacy is more than just reading and writing*, 3/23/2020 https://ncte.org/blog/2020/03/literacy-just-reading-writing/

Rogers, T., Winters, K. L., Perry, M., & LaMonde, A. M. (2015). *Youth, critical literacies and civic engagement: Arts, media, and literacy in the lives of adolescents*. Routledge.

Teitlebaum, K. (2010). Critical civic literacy in schools. Adolescents seeking to understand and improve the(ir) world. In J. DeVitis & L. Irvin-DeVitis (Eds.), *Adolescent education: A reader* (pp. 307–322). Peter Lang.

Truettner, W., & Wallach, A. (1994). *Thomas Cole: Landscape into history*. Yale University Press.

CHAPTER 1

ACT LIKE A TEACHER

Shaping Future Educators Through Drama-Based Pre-Service Pedagogy

Jaydene Elvin and Andy Waldron

Standing in front of a room of 30 blinking sets of eyeballs can be a daunting step on the journey of any teacher. Insecurities, imposter syndrome, and self-doubt can creep into the brain and shake educators to their core. This is similar to shaky nerves that rattle new actors stepping out on a stage in front of an audience. Actors can hide themselves behind their role, put on the physical mask of a confident professional, speak with strength and authority, and present a compelling, compassionate character to the viewer... and so can teachers. Are educators all that different from performers? Perhaps readers, like the two of us, have been accused of using the "teacher voice" during a heated game night or giving a loved one the "teacher look." The roles that educators put on in order to teach is more than just code-switching; it is a putting-on of a role, a persona to engage with youth with more compassion and patience than perhaps we have in our daily lives.

Effective teaching requires the confidence and communicative skills to stand up in front of groups of people, as well as the flexibility to respond to the unexpected. Similarly, engaging in a democratic pedagogical process involves carefully listening to diverse communities, reflecting, and responding in authentic ways. Drama and acting require these same skills, and it is no surprise that teaching is often compared to acting on a stage (Tauber & Mester, 2007). Combining drama strategies with pre-service teacher training benefits young teachers in a variety of ways. This includes cultivating spaces for different perspectives, enhancing student learning, and building confident teachers ready to tackle the challenges of the classroom. Specifically, teachers must develop a teacher persona different to the one they use with friends and family (Carroll, 2002) and use that persona to present subject matter to students. Teachers of Language Arts and Literacy are especially in need of these skills because their content directly involves communications with others. School subjects like writing, public speaking, literature and the core ability to read, are all enhanced by teachers that can present themselves effectively 'onstage' in front of a dry erase board.

While actors learn and develop these essential performance skills through years of training, teachers are often expected to pick them up "on the go." Traditional pre-service teacher training courses often consist of methods courses, observations, and student teaching experiences with a professional mentor that provide "supporting material for this intensive period of reflection and professional development (Crookes, 2003, p.1)." However, we approach these training courses with a drama-based perspective because it is an effective method that empowers students to think critically, develop their teacher persona, confidently engage young people, and build strategies to successfully navigate the changing classroom of tomorrow. These skills, we believe, should be available to all pre-service teachers, regardless of where they currently are in their teaching journey. Democratization of teaching can begin with guiding all hopeful teachers towards openly accessing their voices, bodies, and confidence to tackle the classroom challenges that await them.

This chapter will explore the innovative pedagogical approaches that use rehearsal and performance techniques like movement, voice, improvisation, in teacher training to help pre-service and novice teachers develop essential teaching and delivery skills. The chapter will also cover the importance of integrating reflection in drama-based, cross-curricular teacher training. This chapter is designed to provide pre-service teachers, including those intending to teach English Language Arts (ELA) and literacy, with strategies that they can use to improve their own teaching skills, as well as suggestions for how some of these pedagogical approaches can translate into the classroom.

THE BEGINNING OF THE PROGRAM

Our process involves a drama-based pedagogical approach to teacher-training. We have implemented this program in several spaces including; an undergraduate TESOL (Teaching English to Speakers of Other Languages) practicum course, language arts education courses, theatre education courses, and workshops with preservice elementary and secondary teachers. This drama-based pedagogical approach (referred to Act Like a Teacher, and later Read Like a Teacher, by the authors) came about as a response to comments our first author received from a local Intensive English Program (IEP) in regards to the student-interns having difficulties stepping out of the role of a student and into the role of the teacher. The director of the IEP felt that the student- or pre-service teachers would benefit from some training in drama. As a result, our "Act Like a Teacher" program was born, a program that provided teacher training utilizing acting techniques. It started with the Practicum course and later expanded to workshops at other organizations and universities. In the undergraduate TESOL Practicum, most students were studying to teach ESL to adults in adult schools, community colleges and abroad. A few of them were also intending on working with elementary and high school students in either ESL programs and English classes. Students attending the workshops were either Liberal Studies students or students studying for multiple or single-study credentials in the State of California. Many of our students had no prior experience with drama and we therefore wanted to create a safe space for our students to explore, try out new things and to ultimately take risks that would benefit their learning and development as a teacher.

BUILDING COMMUNITY THROUGH ICEBREAKERS

Few things will elicit a greater collective groan in a department or building meeting than an icebreaker activity. Even teachers feel a bit of consternation when faced with sharing more about themselves through a get-to-know-you activity. It's common for icebreakers, or starter activities, to be perceived as irrelevant, yet they are perhaps among the most underestimated teaching strategies out there. They are essential to the development of community in the classroom because they set the tone. Getting students on the right wavelength for the learning strategies of the day can be achieved through these starter activities (Herrman, 2015). For our Practicum course and subsequent workshops, we knew that we would be implementing a drama-based pedagogy, and this could potentially be uncomfortable and overwhelming for some pre-service teachers. They signed up for a teacher training course, and not a drama class, and so it was important for us to set the tone of the benefits of drama-based pedagogy right from the get-go. Because we asked our pre-service teachers to step out of their comfort zones and to try something new, it was highly important that we created a space where they felt comfortable with themselves, each other, and the instructor. We needed to ensure a sense of community amongst our preservice teachers. This process began with the use of icebreakers designed to get students out of their comfort zone and to position them in a space for learning. These icebreakers were the first step toward building a sense of community that continued to develop over the course of the training program. The icebreakers we used in our course allowed us to help students achieve that level of comfort right from the beginning. Furthermore, it helped develop group cohesion within the class as the pre-service teachers developed a good rapport with each other and with the instructor.

For our icebreakers, we made sure that they were drama-based and were relatively low risk. We wanted students to step out of their comfort zone a little by trying out the activity, but we did not want the activity to be so far out of their comfort zone that it would cause them stress and anxiety. Our goal as teachers should therefore be to lower the affective filter enough so that students are able to grow, develop and even take risks in their learning. When a student enters the classroom, they bring with them an "affective filter"; an invisible psychological filter (or barrier) that either helps or hinders one's learning experience. The lower the filter–the higher the success. Stress, anxiety, low self-esteem, boredom, lack of motivation are all things that increase the affective filter. A low affective filter results in increased self-confidence and the desire to explore, learn and even take a few risks. Our icebreakers were designed to lower this affective filter and to help participants to develop group cohesion and to get to know one another better. We should add that we did not create nor invent these activities. We brought them in from our own courses that we have taken, taught, and heard about through our professional networks and resources like Viola Spolin's *Theatre Games for the Classroom.*

CHECK-IN ACTIVITY

A staple in our work as teachers is the "Check-In." This activity has the instructor verbally or visually connect with the students in the room and then with each other to gain insight into how the students were feeling. A "feelings" check-in at the beginning of the lesson allowed pre-services teachers the opportunity to gauge the emotional state of the class. For example, we asked the class to make an expression that demonstrates how they are feeling today. These check-ins can be used to lighten the mood, build community and can even be sculpted to align to the curricular content for the day. Questions like; "If you were a tree, what kind of tree would you be?," "If you could have any super-power, which would you have?," or "If money were no object, where would you travel for vacation?" allow the participants to learn more about each other, to connect over things outside of the content area, and to have fun.

THE SHAKE-OUT ACTIVITY

In order to release stress and tension within the participants, we started with simple activities like a group shake-out. The instructor led the students in an activity where they loosened up their muscles and got energized by shaking different parts of their body. This was done quickly with a "take a moment and shake it off" or a more in-depth version where the group collectively can count down from 8 to 1 in this activity. To put this in practice, have the students shake their right hands above their heads 8 times while counting down from 8 to 1. Repeat this step with the left arm, right leg, and left leg. Then start back at the right hand and start at 7. Complete this whole sequence until the class erupts in a delightfully, goofy movement moment of all limbs shaking out on "One, one, one, one." This was very popular in our classes and workshops and became part of our regular warm up routine.

NAME AND ACTION ACTIVITY

Another effective drama-based icebreaker activity was "Name and Action." Here the group learns each other's name by associating it with an action. For example, the teacher started by saying their name and then completing a hula-hoop motion with their hips. The rest of the group repeats the teacher's name and completes the same hula-hoop movement. The next person to the right or left repeated the activity with their own name and a new movement, which the group repeated back. While this activity seems simple, it is quite successful in helping everyone learn each other's names and break down the nervous energy walls around them. This is important as it helps the pre-service teachers to feel like they have connections in the room. From the teacher's point of view, it also allowed assessment to happen. The teacher could see which students were resistant to group participation, assess their English language comprehension skills, observe any physical limitations in their class members, and discover the general attitude to cross-curricular learning.

PARTNER INTRODUCTIONS ACTIVITY

Another good icebreaker that helped students engage in the class community was "Introduce your Partner...In Character." Students were paired off and asked to learn some new information about each other. This allowed students to become mini-experts on each other, practice their listening and speaking skills, and public presentation skills. When they were done, they introduced their partner to the rest of the group, but with a twist–they introduced their partner in character (e.g., a cheerleader, a member of royalty, a car salesperson, etc.). In terms of drama-based pedagogy, this activity pushed students out of their potential comfort zones by having to speak publicly but allowed them the creative shield of doing so with a goofy voice. While the activity involved using character stereotypes, it also made people laugh, shared tidbits about each other, and reduced student anxiety in the space.

ICEBREAKERS LEADING TO A SENSE OF COMMUNITY

These icebreaker activities developed a sense of community, and lowered the affective filter, but pre-service teachers began to see how they could use these activities to set the tone of their own classrooms. The following comment by a student in the Practicum course (taught online during the 2020 Covid pandemic) describes some of the benefits of icebreaker activities.

> We did a few ice-breakers and activities that really allowed me to be more of myself in front of my classmates and it helped us all to learn a lot more than we would have if we all had our cameras off and didn't speak to one another. The affective-filter is extremely important to learning another language, and I will keep this in mind in my own foreign language classes, as well as when I teach ESL. That said, it doesn't just apply to SLAT [Second Language Acquisition Teaching]. It really does apply to learning in general. I can use the activities I learned in this class to help my students come out of their shells and interact with one another. (Student A, LING 171-I, Spring 2021 end of course questionnaire)

So as we can see from above, icebreakers really are beneficial as a first step toward community building and developing a sense of group cohesion. However, to achieve optimal success in both the icebreakers and developing a sense of community in general, the involvement of the teacher is essential. In our program, we found that the more the instructor joined in on these icebreakers and drama-based activities, the more willing pre-service teachers were to let their guard down and participate. The mentality of the practicum students became that of "well if everyone else, including the teacher is giving it a go, then so should I."

In our Practicum course and subsequent workshops, continuous activities were developed to create the sense of community in the classroom. Icebreakers progressed to drama-based activities in movement and voice. By the time we reached improvisation, students were comfortable with each other and very eager to attempt these different activities. This is where we reiterate the importance of progressing from lower risk to more difficult tasks. Had we begun the class with improvisation activities, students may not have been comfortable enough with themselves or one another to try them out (remembering that these students are not drama students and so acting may not come naturally to them). This progression in activities and the community that came as a result really put pre-service teachers into a position whether they felt more confident with their own abilities and were able to support one another through the challenges they encountered, as expressed in the pre-service teacher comment below:

> This course undoubtedly comes with a tight-knit classroom community. Everyone has a moment where they have to come out of their shell for the improv and acting approaches, so, in turn, everyone grows closer to one another as we support each other through the challenges. (Student B–Ling 171 Practicum course, Spring 2021, end of course survey)

The following pre-service teacher comments further highlight the importance of the sense of community that needs to be built in order for a drama-based pedagogy to be successful.

> Something from this course that I will carry with me through my teaching career is undoubtedly the importance of establishing a strong classroom community. Not only did I experience this through our classroom environment and dynamic, but also through the means of how we handle challenges or misunderstandings inside of our own classrooms. As I worked with my students, developing strong relationships and establishing a safe environment where questions and mistakes are welcomed proved to be something that nurtured students' linguistic growth and confidence. (Student D–Ling 171, Spring 2021, end of course survey)

ENGAGING THE MIND

A couple of years ago, an ESL teacher at one of our local ESL programs was going through a difficult time and this began to affect their teaching. Students reported that they felt the teacher was being rude to them, that they didn't care and wasn't really listening to their needs. They expressed that their attempts to engage were shut down and this made them unwilling to participate in future activities. When we observed this teacher, we noted that some days the class was excellent, but yet there were days where they didn't go as well. The issue? It seemed as though the teacher was facing some challenges outside of the classroom and was carrying this baggage into the classroom. We suspect the above situation is not unique. While a curriculum is a blend of the content as well as the pedagogical method used to implement it, it is ultimately presented by a human with real feelings and stresses to consider. Teachers set the tone of the classroom and create the conditions for effective learning. However, all teachers, like students, have bad days, where it can be hard to put aside their outside concerns, put on a "teacher face" and deliver an inspiring lesson. When teachers and students enter a classroom space, they not only carry the negative weight of the day, but also the other classes, work, family pressures, and so forth (as was the case with our teacher described in the scenario above). For this reason, we felt it was best to begin each class session/workshop with a few mindfulness strategies, so that students could take a moment to themselves, to relax and forget about the stresses of the outside world, so that their students wouldn't pick up on any negative energy the teacher might be feeling.

BODY SCAN ACTIVITY

A useful mindfulness activity we used was a "body scan," where the instructor led the pre-service teachers through a self-aware reflection of themselves. The goal of the exercise was to bring mindfulness to physical tension. This encouraged the individual to connect with themselves, release tension, acknowledge pain or discomfort, and address those issues. To begin, we asked participants to lower their tongues from the roofs of their mouths and to shake out their shoulders. These are common tension points that awareness can release. The mindfulness activities often also included targeted massage and release. Pre-service teachers were instructed to select an area of the body that they had noticed during the body-scan that was causing them some discomfort and to massage that area for a short period of time. They could also shake out their limbs, jump up and down, nod and shake their heads, etc. Upon completion of these activities pre-service teachers ideally feel more relaxed, in-tune with their bodies and ready to step into the role of a teacher. We believe that students can read a teacher's nonverbal communication through tension or relaxation (as was the case with the example scenario above), and by bringing our own attention to our own bodies, we can create a more supportive, conducive space for learning.

CHECK IT AT THE DOOR ACTIVITY

A series of "Check it at the door" activities were aimed at helping our pre-service teachers to develop techniques to leave those negative emotions outside. We wanted to put them into a positive mindset, one that would be conducive to learning. As with many drama activities, we began with the breath. The instructor began by leading the class in some deep breathing exercises, which have been known to lower the heart rate, reduce stress and anxiety levels and to increase one's attention span. For example, asked the group to take a deep breath in through the nose and exhale through the mouth. After a few passes, we added a time count. "On four counts, breathe in through the nose, and, for four counts, out through the mouth." We further explained to our pre-service teachers that these breathing exercises can be done at any time, even in the middle of class when they begin to feel their stress and/or anxiety levels increasing. They can also use it with their own students to get them into a learning mindset.

> I constantly have to present in front of large crowds of people for work and/or intimidating, smart, older-than-me men. I have consistently "checked it at the door," been intentional with my body language/breath support, and have even jumped around in a hallway before walking into a conference room (Student E- LING 171, Spring 2021, end of course survey)

ENGAGING THE BODY AND VOICE

One key element of our pre-service teacher training program is to engage the participants in activities that bring greater awareness to their bodies and voices. Specifically, we want these teachers to make informed, intentional choices and reflect on how these decisions can amplify their existing teacher skills. We believe, in order to become better teachers, literacy coaches, presenters, we need to better understand our own bodies. We also reinforced that these physical choices are not inherently bad nor inherently good, but rather they communicate to the students. *Moving like a teacher* involves being aware of what we are doing and making choices to support and encourage our students. Our work with preservice teachers, as well as in our own public speaking, acting, and education classes, has shown us that sometimes showing is often more important than telling.

POSE LIKE A TEACHER ACTIVITY

When it comes to the use of our bodies during presentation moments, little has caused more apprehension than what to do with our hands. Sometimes speakers will enjoy having a podium or piece of paper to grip onto, just to avoid feeling awkward. Rather than let that awkwardness stand, we dove in and brainstormed with the whole group all the various hand-keeping options. Again, this comes back to making intentional, comfortable choices, while keeping in mind the communicative effect this has on our students. Similarly, pre-service teachers often struggle with standing in place without shifting weight and swaying side to side. Rather than simply tell them to stand their ground, we unpacked why our bodies sway and covered strategies for balancing our weight, and added intentional movement into our presentation toolboxes. In practice, this involved the group of students standing in a large circle. We tried out different non-verbal poses and then we asked, after each option, for the students to verbally share what this might communicate to their "audience," their own students. We reinforced that gestures and the way we stand are not inherently good or bad, "they just are." Finally, we over-dramatized the movement. In practice, it would sound like; "shift all of your weight to your right hip. How does that feel? Shift it to the left side. Now pop back and forth. Imagine watching a teacher during a whole class period shifting side-to-side. How might your students perceive that teacher?." We have found that by finding room to laugh about our own body quirks, we can better attend to our students' anxieties about standing in front of others. In the end, by becoming more aware of our postures and non-verbal communication, we can create supportive learning environments.

ENGAGING THE VOICE

The teacher's voice, we believe, is one of the strongest tools in our toolboxes. A whisper can silence the horde and a dynamic plea can inspire them into action. Now, our voices are very personal and tackling how we sound can be quite challenging for actors and educators alike. We focused our attention on a variety of vocal modifications and often put them in opposition to each other, even though they are quite spectral in nature. These included rate (fast vs slow), volume (loud vs soft), pitch (high vs low), and finally vocal energy & emphasis. Again, the focus was not on what is "good or bad" but rather on the vocal choices made and how to best support student engagement through these choices.

WARM-UP SONG ACTIVITY

In order to both reduce the affective filter, to assess student voice and movement skills, and to get students engaged with their vocal power, we often began with song activities like "Boom Chicka Boom." Like the icebreakers described earlier, these engage participants in vocal exploration and also break down their barriers through fun, participatory activities. "Boom Chicka Boom" is a call and response activity and brought together both movement and voice. The lyrics are pretty simple and have students repeating the line after each quoted part; "I said a Boom Chicka Boom" and "I said a Boom, Chicka Rocka, Chicka Rocka, Chicka Boom." The extra layer of fun involves adding or substituting consonant sounds along with physical movement. For example, "Race Car version" involves saying "Vroom Chicka Vroom" and has the physical movement of turning a car wheel or shifting gears. It was a goofy activity to warm-up our participants. Underneath the fun surface and on a learner-centered, pedagogical level, it introduced rhyming words, used physical actions to reinforce denotative meaning, and provided valuable data for individual assessment.

VOCAL PRODUCTION ACTIVITY

Next, in order to better understand how our voices impact our teaching and presentation, we needed to help the pre-service teachers better understand vocal production itself. This began by breaking down the vocal production process to unpack the role of the diaphragm, lungs, vocal chords, neck muscles, and resonators. We narrated the vocal production process, had students physically touch their abdomens, chests, throats, and nasal cavities to feel expansion and contraction, vibration, and resonance. This led us to highlight vocal production challenges that often occur in pre-service teachers. For example, our participants often physically connected louder volume with higher pitch. When asked to speak louder or to project across the room, their voices audibly become higher while also increasing muscle tension in their necks. So, we addressed the problem by pointing it out and then breaking it down. We went through breathing and projecting from the diaphragm and reinforced that the power of our voice comes from the air support itself. After this modification, we practiced projecting across the space with our voices while maintaining relative pitch and energy level.

CREATIVE EMPHASIS ACTIVITY

In order to show students how emphasis can affect meaning, we did an activity where we played with modifications. We began by putting the sentence "She didn't steal my wallet" on the board or projection screen. Next, we had students practice changing their inflection so that each word, in sequence, was emphasized. We then talked through how the meaning shifts based on these vocal changes. Rather than read the sentences aloud in a dull, monotone fashion, we encouraged participants to verbally perform these meaning shifts. For example, with vocal emphasis given in capital letters, "SHE didn't steal my wallet" implied that this female-identifying person didn't do it, someone else did. "She didn't STEAL my wallet" implied that she didn't steal it but rather borrowed it to, perhaps, buy a coffee. We did a similar activity to focus on pauses and pace. We started by writing on the board the following quote from Daniel Kahneman, "Nothing in life is as important as you think it is, while you are thinking about it." We then broke down and demonstrated how the pace of the reading impacts the understanding of the content. If one rushes through the line, ignoring punctuation and the rhythm, it can be difficult to absorb the true meaning. Each of these skills were approached from both a language arts, meaning shifting perspective *and through* an enhanced drama performance lens.

PUTTING TALK INTO (PRACTICED) ACTION: READ-ALOUDS

One of the strongest literacy acts we can do for youth is to read-aloud and demonstrate things like book handling skills, methods for encountering new words, using context clues to unpack meaning, and share our own love of reading. Informing our work is Jim Trelease's book, *The Read Aloud Handbook*, is an amazing resource that we highly recommend to our own students. Reading aloud also combines skills in both verbal performance and physical delivery. As described later in the chapter, we practice using the range of our voices to help emphasize key narrative elements, enhance the story, and engage youth. We began our instruction on the physical act of reading aloud by first putting students' minds at ease about their own reading voices and presentation skills. Often, pre-service teachers may not have had experience reading to young people, so sitting in front of that many eyes can be daunting. We also reinforced that read alouds can (and should) be done for students of all ages. Finally, we then broke the whole process down into voice, as described earlier in the chapter, and body movement. For example, we physically demonstrated all the different ways to hold the book during a read-aloud. Teachers do not need to be able to read upside-down or read from the side. We can turn our heads any way we want, read the book while it faces us and then turn to share it with our students. Pre-service teachers, in our experience, can get caught up in what it is "supposed to look like" and feel limited by that. The physical / vocal choices that teachers make can impact the ways youth engage with the content and learn to read.

In terms of content delivery, we also emphasized and demonstrated the use of adding active points of participation, especially for younger learners. These are moments when the teacher stops reading and asks predictive or analytical questions of the audience, engages the group in choral speaking or repetition moments, or sign-posts key concepts or ideas. Typically, all students are more engaged by dynamic read-aloud choices as compared to flat, monotone delivery. Yet, even with a flat delivery, they are still hearing the words come alive through the teacher's voice. These techniques can be modified for youth of all ages. With secondary students, for example, one of the authors had an amazing experience reading the first one or two chapters aloud of ten different young adult literature novels to middle school Language Arts classes. The students took notes about each and then after the two weeks of read-alouds, the students got to pick which book they wanted to continue to read. Not only did this engage the students and provided learning choices, but it also exposed them to a variety of writers and voices. Their points of participation were grounded more around character, plot, prediction, and "which stories do you want to read more of?" The reading aloud technique is a true marriage of performance skills with Language Arts and literacy development. Youth are being positively engaged in reading through a dynamic teacher sharing a text. The teacher is actively using sign-posting, analysis, points of participation, and collective storytelling to enhance literacy and reading skills. Finally, it shows that reading is fun and can be a joyful experience.

PUTTING TALK INTO (PRACTICED) ACTION: ROLE-PLAY

The original purpose of our Act Like a Teacher Practicum course and pre-service teacher training workshops was initially to help students step into the role of a teacher. We did this by implementing drama-based pedagogical strategies that helped students learn to move, speak and think like a teacher, by the end of the class they are able to begin to "act" like one too. Our pre-service teachers stepped into the role of a teacher through specific classroom management role plays. To role-play is to temporarily transform oneself into a different person, put themselves in someone else's place, and use body and voice to portray that character. To play a role successfully one needs to temporarily become someone else (Tauber & Meser, 2007, pp. 83–84). Role-play provides pre-service teachers with an excellent opportunity to safely practice skills learned about in class, to develop their teacher persona, and apply the skills they have learned through movement, voice and improvisation. Like read-alouds, role playing is a strong fusion of drama-based practices with pre-service teacher pedagogy. Teachers aren't often provided training in handling challenging student situations when studying to become a teacher, which can lead to anxiety walking into a class for the first time. Role-playing provides a safe zone to try out techniques before entering the real-world.

In our course we decided to create role-plays and teacher demonstrations that centered around classroom management of challenging teaching situations. In these guided-role plays, pre-service teachers practiced teaching content by presenting a mini lesson to their peers. These mini-lessons ranged from listening and speaking activities to activities designed to teach reading, writing. In other words, not only were they practicing classroom management, they were also preparing lessons in TESOL, language arts, and literacy curricular content. Our students/pre-service teachers were informed that as they presented, they would be met with a challenging student situation that they would need to manage . Typically only one or two students were chosen to play the role of a challenging student, while the rest of the class were asked to participate normally. These challenging student situations included students with; an incomprehensible accent, an over-enthusiastic demeanor, and comprehension issues. Other situations were a little more subtle, such as a student who would nod as though they understood the material but did not actually understand; requiring additional assessment.

While "classroom management" may conjure images of rowdy or difficult students, these guided role plays helped our pre-service teachers realize that these challenging situations aren't always going to be "bad students." These are simply situations that a teacher might not know how to best handle. For example, during a read-aloud a teacher might encounter a really enthusiastic student who is unknowingly dominating the entire activity. Therefore, the teacher is faced with the challenge of engaging the entire class in the read-aloud activity, while being careful not to not to dismiss the "challenging student" overenthusiasm. Based on the feedback from the pre-service teachers who have taken the Practicum course and participated in our workshops, these guided role plays/teacher demonstrations proved to be the most valuable. Students did not necessarily know what challenge they were going to be faced with, so they really had to take the skills that they had learned and think on the spot to be able to handle the challenge.

A key element of these guided roleplays/teacher demonstrations was the student-led debrief that immediately followed. During the debrief the class the role play/demonstration covering topics such as what went well, what they would do differently and so forth. The focus of this discussion included the content and materials and how they were presented. They also commented on how the teacher handled the challenging situation and brainstormed ideas and strategies to manage those classroom situations in the future. As students became comfortable debriefing and sharing with one another, they then began to seek advice from their peers pertaining to other situations they had either experienced in the classroom or during observations.

CONCLUSION

While our chapter has predominantly focused on the use of drama skills in teacher training, as previously mentioned, many of these activities can also be used in the classroom to teach content, such as language and literacy. Farmer (2011) explains that drama can be considered a close ally in literacy development. In fact, he states that speaking and listening skills can be enhanced through drama strategies, improvisation, role-play, and through the exchange of information and negotiation that develop out of group work. Writing skills can be developed as new dialogue is created by students and improvisation and story-telling can help students understand narrative structures (Farmer, 2011, p.3). In our chapter we discussed a sample of icebreakers that we used to build community among our pre-service teachers in our Practicum course and workshops, but they can also be adapted to build community within a younger audience. The student check-in activities provide the teacher with insight to the current emotional state of their students. Students can learn about stress and emphasis in language through the creative emphasis activity. Literacy can further be developed through the read-alouds that help students develop a sense of the world and allows them to develop their comprehension and vocabulary skills. Role-play can further enable students to explore contrasting viewpoints, travel in time and place, and with teachers participating in this process by offering challenging viewpoints, this can stimulate thought and lively discussion among students (Farmer, 2011, p.16).

Preparing our future educators for the classroom and the challenges they will face therein, is a tough task—our understatement of the year. We strongly believe that if new teachers can think of themselves as being on a stage, they can better engage the young people around them in their literacy development. The art of teaching is a series of intentional choices to craft the learning environment to best serve our students and this begins with crafting our own delivery skills. Teachers hone their voices and bodies to help our students engage with the content. As we present these courses/workshops, we model confidence and passion through our delivery and can inspire future leaders to do the same. Our workshops often involve us sharing our own struggles, using our own bodies and voices as teaching tools, and supporting the participants to reflect on their own. It is not easy to turn the mirror on ourselves, but by adding a bit of fun, breaking down the barriers to full participation, and giving concrete tools for our participants to use, we can democratize the teaching process. We hope that by doing this, our pre-service teachers will be able to draw connections to how they may be able to implement the strategies learned within their own classrooms in order to connect with their own students. Contrary to popular opinion, teaching is not a field just for extroverts or those already skilled in speaking with others. For those who have a passion for education and working with youth, but lack the confidence or skills to engage effectively, the use of drama in teacher training will help them enhance their presentation skills and develop confidence in their teaching abilities. When faced with a challenging task like speaking to a room of new students, try putting on the character of an amazing teacher. How does that amazing teacher stand? Speak? Engage with their students? We don't believe in "fake it 'til you make it" but rather "act like a teacher to become a teacher."

REFERENCES

Carroll, C. (2002, April 15). Getting good teaching evaluations without stand-up comedy. *The Chronicle of Higher Education*. Retrieved from http://chronicle.com/jobs/2002/04/2002041501c.htm

Crookes, G. (2003). *A practicum in TESOL: Professional development through teaching practice*. Cambridge University Press.

Farmer, D. (2011). *Learning through drama in the primary years*. Drama Resource.

Jennings, P. A., & Greenberg, M. T. (2009). The prosocial classroom: Teacher social and emotional competence in relation to student and classroom outcomes. *Review of Educational Research, 79*(1), 491–525.

King, J., & Ng, K. Y. S. (2018). Teacher emotions and the emotional labour of second language teaching. In *Language Teacher Psychology* (pp. 141–157). Multilingual Matters.

Spolin, V. (1986). *Theater games for the classroom: A teacher's handbook*. Northwestern University Press.

Tauber, R. T., & Mester, C. S. (2007). *Acting lessons for teachers: Using performance skills in the classroom* (Vol. 38). Greenwood Publishing Group.

Trelease, J. (2013). *The read-aloud handbook*. (7th ed.). Penguin Books.

CHAPTER 2

BUILDING A PHOTOGRAPHIC TEACHING PHILOSOPHY

ELA Preservice Teachers' Journey to See the Unseen

Pamela Hartman and Dani Tinkel

> *In order to arrive at what you are not*
> *You must go through the way in which you are not,*
> *And what you do not know is the only thing you know*
> *And what you own is what you do not own*
> *And where you are is where you are not.*
> —T. S. Eliot, "East Coker" (*The Four Quartets*)

In the first week of my Introduction to Teaching English in Secondary Schools course, I tell my English Language Arts (ELA) preservice teachers (PSTs) that they will need to uncover what they believe about education. These beliefs include those about the roles of teachers and students, what should be taught, and how teaching and learning should take place. Additionally, I indicate that they should investigate how they came to these beliefs. I emphasize that it is important that they see what previously may have been unseen or unexamined in order to organize and confront their educational beliefs and histories. This process of examination is important because education researchers have found that past experiences and life histories can positively or negatively affect how preservice teachers will teach in the future (Britzman, 1992; Connelly and Clandinin, 1988; Knowles, 1992; Lortie, 2002).

In this class, I also introduce the idea that, as preservice teachers, they are entering a profession whose members must question commonly (and uncommonly) held beliefs about education, whether those beliefs are held within the profession or by society. Studies have shown that media and popular culture are saturated with representations of schools and teachers and that our perceptions of education are highly influenced by these encounters (Bulman, 2015; Cohen and Scheer, 1997; Dalton, 2010; Harris, 2009; Heilman, 2001; Joseph and Burnaford, 2001; Labaree, 2000; Liston and Renga, 2014; Lortie, 2002; Shoffner, 2016; Weber and Mitchell, 1995).

For this reason, preservice, as well as practicing teachers, need to critically reflect on what they see rather than passively consume it. One of my goals for my PSTs is that they not only better understand the complexity of education, but also engage with these complexities as active members of the teaching profession. Preservice teachers need to feel empowered to meet the challenges of education rather than becoming overwhelmed by them. In order to do so, they need to develop an informed and well-interrogated philosophy of education.

In our ELA program, all PSTs are required to construct a philosophy of education, both for their introductory course and for their student teaching application. Traditionally, PSTs produce these as short, written statements. However, I have found that PSTs often fall into repeating vague and cliché ideas that they do not often critique. Their position statements could fit almost any PST or practicing ELA teacher. Yes, they all love English. They all love kids and think they can learn. But what makes them as teachers different? How do they approach the classroom differently than others? I decided that I needed to approach this task differently. I needed my PSTs to see themselves as the teachers they are and could be. I needed them to better reflect on their perceptions and beliefs about education and on the origins of those beliefs. I also needed them to find ways to get underneath the beliefs that had been simply laid upon them assumptions they had not recognized or confronted. I decided that I needed to bring more artistic response into my teacher education courses.

ARTISTIC RESPONSE AND LITERACY

Artistic response is the process by which readers create concrete representations of their transactions with a text through artistic means, including visual arts (e.g., drawing, sculpture, photography, and painting), drama, and music (Hartman, Berg, Schuler, and Knauer, 2019). Educators and scholars have found artistic response can be an effective way to teach literacy (Chicola and Smith, 2005; Grant, 2008; Holdren, 2012; Macro and Zoss, 2019; Miller and Hopper, 2010; Sidelnick and Svoboda, 2000; Wilhelm, 2016). These strategies provide opportunities for students to engage with texts and use aesthetic and narrative thinking to organize and express their learning. In doing so, students acquire new understandings and ways of thinking.

Expressing ideas visually can be a particularly effective way for students to analyze complex concepts. Researchers have found that students who interpret and transform what they think into different forms, including textually and visually, demonstrate higher levels of understanding of both content and textual form. (Beach, Campano, Edmiston, & Borgmann, 2010; Dunn, 2021; Hartman, Berg, Fulton, and Schuler, 2021). For instance, in her study of her college-level methods class, Patricia Dunn (2021) found that preservice teachers were better able to analyze complex concepts when they represented them in a drawn image. Producing images challenged PSTs to think more deeply about the critical aspects of the concept and how they could effectively communicate their ideas. In addition, Dunn found that preservice teachers benefitted from sharing their ideas, both orally and in writing, with their peers because they could compare renderings of similar concepts. For these reasons, I brought more artistic response strategies into my methods courses, particularly when preparing my PSTs to develop their philosophies of education.

PHOTOGRAPHIC PHILOSOPHY PROJECT

To start the process of building their philosophies of education, PSTs need to reflect on their current beliefs about education and to consider how their beliefs are influenced by their personal experiences and encounters with media and pop culture. To do so, I incorporate a series of activities throughout the semester. These activities included examining critical moments in their experience in schools; analyzing influential representations of teachers and teaching in film, television, and other media; and looking at historical events (e.g., school shootings) and educational movements (e.g., high-stakes testing) that have affected education today. These activities culminate in PSTs creating a Photographic Philosophy project. For this project, PSTs think metaphorically about teaching ELA in secondary schools and represent these ideas through original digital photographs. I based this project on a sample assignment described in Janet Alsup's book *Teacher Identity Discourses: Negotiating Personal and Professional Spaces* (2005). Throughout this project and the sequence of teaching methods that lead up to it, I challenge PSTs to critically examine experiences and events that may shape their beliefs about education today and how some of their beliefs might compete and even conflict with one another. I also ask each of them to consider how they might address these issues as they prepare to become a teacher. The focus of this chapter is how I teach PSTs to use artistic strategies as preparation for the type of thinking necessary for this assignment.

RE-EVALUATING THE PROJECT

After teaching this assignment for several semesters, I revised my approach to the Photographic Philosophy project with the help of an undergraduate student intern who had previously taken the course. I frequently invite PSTs who are further along in the program to intern. Each semester, the interns not only mentor the newer PSTs, but also help me to improve the course. This work has included developing more effective lessons and creating new, and often more meaningful, assignments. Dani had demonstrated both an insight in her coursework and an ability to mentor other PSTs. She also expressed a strong interest in artistic response and how to effectively utilize these methods. For these reasons, I invited her to intern with this class and to help me investigate ELA preservice teachers' perceptions about using art and artistic strategies as a tool for teaching and learning. Additionally, we wanted to use this knowledge to reflect on artistic strategies implemented in this class and perhaps to revise the Photographic Philosophy project.

To begin, Dani and I examined the various activities and assignments and whether they were effective in meeting the goals of the course. Dani indicated that the most interesting part for her was creating the Photographic Philosophy. However, she divulged that, despite feeling as though it was one of the most impactful assignments, she was not satisfied with her final product. While she had an overall plan for what she wanted to communicate, she found it challenging to dig into the complexities of her thinking and to express them visually. She said that this dissatisfaction was amplified when she saw other PSTs' projects, which she often perceived to have more depth and to be more engaging.

As we discussed the Photographic Philosophy project and Dani's experience further, we examined projects from previous semesters. We noticed that their quality varied greatly, both in substance and form. While a range of quality is to be expected on any assignment, we wondered if PSTs sometimes struggled because of their lack of previous experience using artistic response strategies for thinking and learning. If they did have this experience in previous classes, we wondered if these were meaningful experiences and if they influenced PSTs's attitudes about their use for instruction. We also asked ourselves, is there a better way to break down the thinking necessary to complete the project?

To gauge PSTs's experience with and attitudes about artistic response strategies, we developed and administered a presurvey at the start of the semester. Most PSTs expressed through their presurvey that they valued the arts and participated in them during their secondary school experience. Their ELA teachers also incorporated some fine arts activities into their lessons. However, this incorporation was limited to drawing and creative writing. When the arts were used by their former ELA teachers, PSTs said that they usually found these activities effective. In fact, they claimed that the lessons were more engaging and memorable and that these opportunities provided more independence for them to explore their ideas. Most PSTs were considering using the fine arts in their future classrooms. We were surprised that one student even said that "I want to show that literacy comes through in many forms, not just words. To be literate is not only knowing how to read and write, but it's also knowing how to interpret in your own eyes."

Although PSTs expressed an interest in incorporating the arts in their future classrooms, they admitted that they were not completely sure about how to integrate them. With these surveys in mind, we decided to consciously include more artistic response activities and assignments throughout the semester. In addition, we expanded the instruction behind the Photographic Philosophy to include more modeling and guided practice. Specifically, we identified that 1) we needed to more thoroughly break down the thinking and skills needed to complete the Photographic Philosophy in our instruction. This instruction included teaching PSTs how to *read* photographs in order for them to create meaningful projects. It also included cultivating habits of mind by which PSTs would seek out the complexities and contradictions in the images they both read and created, which we hoped would lead to more unique and thoughtful teaching philosophies. 2) We needed to be more deliberate in explaining our pedagogy. By uncovering the choices that we made in our instruction, we hoped that PSTs would see the thinking required of us as teachers and be better equipped to replicate this process. In this chapter, we provide a detailed description of how we used artistic methods to help our PSTs develop their Photographic Philosophies.

READING PHOTOS AND PHOTOGRAPHIC PROJECTS

To continue to support our PSTs's journeys to build more introspective personal teaching philosophies, at the midpoint of the semester, I required them to complete a Photographic Philosophy with a partner. This artistic response strategy challenged many PSTs to leave their comfort zones and to think more deeply about their ideas about education and how to express them. It also required PSTs to think more metaphorically, which helped to uncover culturally negotiated understandings about teaching and learning and how they are represented around us. Educational researchers have found that this kind of metaphoric thinking about complex concepts can be an effective teaching strategy because using "a sign or symbol can evoke complex and often culturally mediated understandings which can be both presentational and discursive.... Thus the association between the sign [symbol], the signified[,] and the signifier generates endless ways of representing events, objects or concepts, or ways of creating meaning potential" (Ruth Crick and Kath Grushka 450). In other words, when PSTs practice metaphoric thinking, they learn to apply their personal experiences and cultural knowledge to better express their complex and growing understandings. To prepare PSTs to engage with this type of thinking when composing their own Photographic Philosophies, we first needed to teach them to analyze, or read, photographs. Quite simply, PSTs needed to know what to look for. This process meant learning to uncover the complexity of the images and the contradictions that might be present.

Instruction began with examining two sample photos, both taken from previously completed projects (Figure 2.1 and Figure 2.2). These photos, one displaying a compass and the other a wooden bridge, originally

Figure 2.1

included brief written analyses that explained the meaning the creators were trying to convey. We removed these analyses so that PSTs could freely explore the photos and come to their own conclusions without the influence of creators' claims.

First, we modeled the thinking required for this task by analyzing the composition of the photo displaying the compass (Figure 2.1). We pointed out that the photo contains not only a compass, but also an outstretched arm and a hand holding it. We explained that these images stood out to us partly because of the dark color of the jacket and compass, which contrasted with the concrete that seemed to serve as a backdrop to the picture, and partly because the hand and compass were towards the center of the photo, which seemed to indicate that they were the focus of the composition. We also said that the way the arm and compass were positioned created a strong line that directed our attention to travel beyond the photo itself. We began to imagine where the person might be looking and what was holding their attention. Since compasses are traditionally used to orient oneself and guide the user to another destination, we concluded that the person seemed focused and determined to reach their destination. This conclusion was further supported because of the strong line created in the image.

When analyzing and taking photos, we pointed out that it is often useful to examine them from different angles, or perspectives, and to decide how each element functions to communicate to their audience a particular purpose. We asked the PSTs to imagine that the person taking the photo is a teacher who is trying to communicate a perspective about education. What effect did this new lens have on their interpretation of the photo? What did they think the creator might be trying to express? In addition, what details or elements of the photo led them to their conclusions?

PSTs took a few minutes to consider their answers and to free-write about them before we opened the floor for full classroom discussion. Multiple PSTs quickly suggested that the compass photo might convey how teachers can act as "guides" for their students. They also noted that they had to work together to reach their destination. One student added that you can't just pick up a compass and "follow" it. In order for the trip to be successful, the holder of the compass has to have, or be given, knowledge about how compasses work.

Our class continued this activity by next considering the photo of the bridge (Figure 2.2). This photo proved to be more challenging to interpret than the first. PSTs identified the bridge, which connects two unseen points, as the central focus. They hypothesized that the bridge represented how teachers connect their students to their learning destination, remarking that "the teacher *is* the bridge!" and teachers "help kids transition through [or travel across] the education program."

Figure 2.2

PSTs also noted the multicolored posts on the bridge. However, they debated if this element was accidental or intentional and, if intentional, what the colors might indicate. They concluded that the colors must be important since they were so dominant in the photo. Unknown to my PSTs, the original creators had explained in their written description, "A classroom must value and respect all of the [students] that reside within and treat them all equally while simultaneously embracing the inherent differences that make the world beautiful and unique." Without reading this text, a student picked up on this idea while considering the photo, arguing that teachers "support" their students who come from diverse backgrounds. He continued, stating that teachers should create an environment of "inclusivity," and by working together [with their students], they form a community.

Through this initial practice, PSTs became comfortable "transacting" (Rosenblatt) with the photos, or texts. While considering what the creators, who were also just starting out in the ELA program, might have intended, they drew on their own knowledge as well as the details of the photos themselves to foster their own interpretations.

At this point, we moved on to analyzing three additional photos in breakout groups. The first photo (not shown) contains an image of a girl wearing a flowy white dress, looking at her reflection in a pond. The second shows a spider in a web (Figure 2.3), and the third image is composed of a girl holding an apple (Figure 2.4). Similar to the previous activity, these photos became progressively harder to interpret because the images themselves were more complex and abstract. We placed PSTs in small groups in order for them to gain more control and independence in the analyzing process, while retaining the support of multiple peers. They recorded their ideas on separate Google Doc tables so that we could monitor their progress and

Figure 2.3

Figure 2.4

only provide support as needed and so that they could analyze the photos without the influence of other groups.

When the groups came back together as a class to share their hypotheses, most noticed that the girl in the pond was looking at her "reflection" in the water and that the creators might be saying that this image represents the need for teachers to be reflective practitioners. One student went further by saying, "It may be a reach, but the water might represent the students.

The girl, or teacher, then, reflects her philosophy [of teaching ELA] onto her students." Overall, PSTs found the photo engaging and stated that they thought it conveyed its message effectively. However, a student commented that "it's a little hard to find the reflection because it's not the main focus of the image." She suggested that the photo could be reshot with this adjustment in mind. Another student asked, "Why not use a mirror?" The class agreed, however, that they appreciated the creativity of the image.

Regarding the photo of the spider, all groups responded that the web was the most significant aspect. However, they failed to come to a consensus as to what it might symbolize. One group said that the web illustrated the need for the teacher to "weave multiple...complex ideas together." Another concluded that the photo suggested that "it's the teacher's job to make sure that the student doesn't get stuck on a topic or in a 'web.'" The final group's conclusion was closer to the creators' intended larger meaning. The creators claimed that their image conveyed the idea of "support," arguing that teachers need to "establish [themselves] as a support system" so that students can learn and feel safe in their classrooms. They continued that the web connects the students in a learning community and that "their ideas are intertwin[ed]." When we asked the class how they thought the photo could be improved, PSTs said they would change the color scheme from black and white to something brighter and more positive looking and less ominous. They explained that the black and white scheme seemed to contradict the intended message. They also indicated that by making this change, the spider could stand out more, thus making the spider, or the teacher, the prominent feature of the composition.

The final photo of the girl with the apple presented the most challenging for PSTs. PSTs confessed that their groups had not come to any final conclusions and that they needed assistance. Each group, however, had made some hypotheses concerning different aspects of the photo, including the apple and the girl's expression. They knew that the apple had something to do with education or teaching and that the girl might represent a teacher, but they were perplexed by her gloomy demeanor. They questioned whether she was "distressed," "exhausted," or, perhaps, "resentful" and what this meant for the image's overall meaning. At this point, we revealed that the idea the creators were going for was "transformation," meaning that teaching should lead to students' growth and ultimately be "transformational." This revelation, however, did not satisfy the PSTs. They said that, while the photo was definitely "artistic," it did not convey this meaning clearly. They also debated whether a teacher could simultaneously desire to be transformational and still hold a negative view of education, especially in light of the country's current political climate. Ultimately, a boisterous discussion of possible revisions ensued. Several PSTs suggested that the creators could have used a model with a more pleasant expression to indicate that this was a positive aspect of teaching. Another student argued that it was problematic that an eaten apple did not clearly indicate the idea of "transformation." They said a more obvious way to represent "transformation" could have been to carve the apple into a sculpture or to bake it into a pie. The student continued, saying that the creators could have even used two side-by-side images, with an apple on one side and a transformed apple on the other.

As indicated by their comments in class and on their post-evaluation, PSTs found that analyzing and debating about the photos was thought-provoking, and they recognized that former PSTs put careful consideration into their images. They also commented that they particularly enjoyed discussing how the creators could have better communicated their message.

The last part of our teaching sequence required PSTs to analyze an entire photographic philosophy. The project that we used, entitled "Threads of Education," featured four photos, including images of a ladder, multiple-colored pencils and crayons, a bulletin board, and two people tied up in strings (see Figure 2.5). These images represented "scaffolding,"

Figure 2.5

"diversity," "connection," and "communication." It also incorporated two connecting components, including a red/brown/white color scheme and a red string, which appears in every photo. In addition to analyzing each individual photo, we asked PSTs to consider how the photos connected with each other to create an overall meaning, or theme, for the project as a whole and to record conclusions and evidence on a Google Doc. PSTs completed this activity in their small groups, and, again, we followed this with a whole class discussion. All groups were able to make meaning of most of the pictures, and our group discussion served to create a richer class understanding of each photo. They identified the red string as being an important element of the photo and hypothesized that it may represent "connection" or "connectivity." They said that the string bonds teachers and students into a learning community, and they argued that teachers have the responsibility through the way they teach to develop this connectivity. Overall, the groups' conclusions were in accordance with the creators' explanation of their project. The creators had argued, "Every [individual] can add something to the classroom and the teaching of the material.... all of them are united by and learning from one another in the classroom."

During the next class, we provided PSTs with specific project guidelines and assigned PSTs to a partner.

THE PROJECT

Besides taking original digital photographs that metaphorically represented their respective beliefs about teaching and learning, PSTs were required to write brief explanations to "unpack" or explain the main metaphorical thinking behind each of the images and the project as a whole. Because the Photographic Philosophy assignment combines both visual and textual response, it offers PSTs a creative and effective way to gain new and richer understandings of their beliefs about education.

For this project, we purposefully assigned each student to work with a partner. In previous classes, we found that PSTs were often challenged by the conceptual thinking needed for this somewhat complex activity. Additionally, we formed each group so that it consisted of PSTs who possessed different, complementary strengths. For instance, we paired PSTs with good speaking skills with PSTs with good writing skills, and we paired PSTs who demonstrated concrete and linear thinking with PSTs who seemed to think more abstractly. We also took PSTs' personalities into consideration because we wanted the groups to work in a constructive and balanced manner. For instance, we avoided pairing dominant PSTs with those who were more reserved and accommodating.

Once the groups were assigned, PSTs took responsibility outside of class for planning and completing the various tasks, such as taking the photos, composing the texts, and editing. While they occasionally asked questions in class or via email, at this point, they mostly worked independently, which seemed to indicate their growth in their knowledge and confidence. After about two and a half weeks, PSTs submitted their final products to Canvas and presented them in class.

The completed Photographic Philosophies featured a wide variety of themes and visuals to represent PSTs' beliefs about education. For the purposes of this report we have included samples of individual photos, from two different projects, and a complete project in order to show the range of the themes and visual representations that the PSTs incorporated.

BUILDING A COMMUNITY

One group's overarching theme was the importance of "building a community" in their future classrooms. The PSTs identified four key components of community–support, communication, accommodation, and inclusivity– that must be achieved and then represented each component in a photo. They symbolized their ideas about "support" by building a Lego tower (Figure 2.6). The Lego tower depicted two Lego people at the top of the tower and one Lego person at the base. The Lego pieces that made up the tower had words like "together," "aid," and "team" taped to their sides. The group explained that the supportive Lego tower reflected both their individual concept of support and their overall theme because "each of the Legos rely on

Figure 2.6

one another in order to build upwards." They wrote, "The adult (teacher) at the bottom right corner sets the foundation in order to help the students at the top [of the tower]. All the words attached to the blocks describe how students and teachers must [work together to] build a community of support." For instance, students and teachers must all "aid" each other to be successful.

During their class presentation, the group, in a kind of "ah-ha" moment, went deeper into their thinking than they originally expressed in the written portion of their project, stating, "This photo represents how teachers and students support each other. Each of the Legos rely on one another in order to build upwards." Therefore, "building a community is not only the teacher's responsibility but also the students'.... Whether [this support] be emotional, physical, or academic, it is vital that students lean on each other." Reflecting on their project led them to new insights.

NOURISH THE MINDS

Another group focused their project on the need for teachers to "nourish the minds" of their future students through communication, creativity, organization, accommodation, and attention to diversity. In order to represent this type of "nourishment," they picked items that college students are very familiar with—food. While food is a rather literal interpretation of "nourishment," the group applied their ideas in interesting and original ways.

For example, when representing the aspect of "creativity," they presented a bagel cut into four sections (Figure 2.7) The group stated that the teacher should divide the bagel, or their instruction, into separate sections

Figure 2.7

and prepare them in different ways to reflect that students have different preferences and nutritional (i.e., educational) needs. Therefore, one type of bagel might not work for every student and options must be provided by the teacher, or server. Each fourth represented different students' "perfect bagel." For instance, a "cream cheese bagel [in the lower left-hand corner] is common and many people love them... but not every student wants/can eat a cream cheese bagel." Perhaps instead, the peanut butter and apple bagel in the lower right corner or the peanut butter and jam bagel, shown in the upper right corner, would better suit other students' needs and preferences. "As educators, we must be able to channel all of our students' varying ideas, beliefs, and levels of creativity to foster a good learning environment." One student's perfect bagel may be an open-ended writing prompt, while another student's perfect bagel may be a more guided assignment. Educators need to acknowledge that each student has unique nutritional needs, and they need to be thoughtful in developing their lesson plans and assignments.

After listening to this group explain the importance of creativity to nourish their students, it became evident to us that "creativity" was another way for this group to describe differentiation. Because this was an entry-level education course, our PSTs did not yet possess the professional vocabulary to express this concept. However, through this project, we could see that they understood and valued the need for differentiation in their future classrooms.

A TRUNK OF SUPPORT WILL HELP OUR STUDENTS BRANCH OUT

As an example of a completed project, we selected a Photographic Philosophy, titled "A Trunk of Support Will Help Our Students Branch Out" (Figure 2.8). The creators metaphorically represented their philosophy of teaching by using images of trees and tree-related objects. They argued that, overall, teachers must provide an environment of support for their students in order for them to succeed in their learning. This support, they said, includes elements of "connection," "challenge," "trust," and "creativity." Additionally, while each element is equally important in its own right, they form the necessary structure, or support, that all students need to thrive.

To represent "connection," the group included an example of tree roots, claiming that the roots connect the tree, or student, to the nutrients for their education. This includes their background knowledge and experiences. The group also included a photo of a bird's nest to represent "trust," since the birds must trust the tree branches to support their home, and students must trust their teachers to create a safe learning environment. The meaning of the final photo, featuring the origami swan, however, was

32 ▪ P. HARTMAN and D. TINKEL

Introduction
As future teachers, we need to support students so they can properly gain the knowledge that they need to succeed in and out of school. We can create this support by connecting our lessons to their lives and by challenging them in their learning. In addition, we must develop trust in the classroom so that students feel protected, and we need to use creativity to engage our students.

We use trees in this project to represent our teaching philosophy. This is because the different aspects of a tree, including its roots, trunk, branches, and products, are helpful to understand our ideas.

Connection

Making connections between students' interests and backgrounds and the new content and skills that we, as teachers, want them to know is important. Much like a tree's roots, students' experiences provide nutrients and support for learning. As the tree needs nutrients for the trunk to develop and grow, students need connections to their own lives to thrive. It is also important for us to understand where our students are coming from. Making these connections will help us tailor our lessons to their individual needs and help them explore difficult topics that we might encounter, such as race or sexuality. By forming these connections, students will be able to better engage with our lessons and grow.

Challenge

As teachers, it is important for us to challenge our students. While some students might need more support, every student needs a challenge in order to reach their full potential. Much like a tree, the trunk represents the basic knowledge. The branches represent more difficult destinations and will push students who require that extra challenge to stay engaged in the learning process.

Trust

By creating trust between us and our students, we can better support their learning. They must trust us to provide a safe environment where they feel secure. In this way, students will feel more confident about engaging with challenging ideas and more comfortable in sharing their thoughts. In the photo of the nest, the birds trust the branches of the bush to support and protect them from harm. Therefore, they have faith in building their nest.

Creativity

As teachers, we need to consider creativity when making lessons or assignments for our students. Creative lessons engage students more, encourage them to make more of an effort, and help students to remember the knowledge that they learned in class. Creative assignments also help support learning by encouraging students to think in new ways and to form new knowledge. For example, while our paper swan came from the tree, it was reshaped and developed into something new. As teachers we want to give our students opportunities to take what they have learned and apply it in new and interesting ways.

Conclusion
While there are many important aspects of being an effective teacher, in our opinion, the most important ones include making connections, providing challenges, building trust, and including creativity. These aspects can be encapsulated by the theme of support.

We believe that we can become a supporting force in our students' education if we reinforce these concepts in our teaching. By doing so, we can help our students succeed in both school and life.

Figure 2.8

not as straightforward as the other photos. The group claimed that it represented "creativity" and that teachers need to incorporate creative lessons to engage students and to encourage them "to think in new ways and to form new knowledge." The paper swan's relationship to the tree wasn't as obvious to us at first glance, but the group explained that it is a product of the tree, or the students' education. The tree is "reshaped and developed into something new." They argued that an educator's goal should be to empower students to employ their knowledge in ways that are meaningful to them. They then confessed that, at the start of their work on the project, they had not considered this last point to be the end goal of a student's education. They said that this struck them as they progressed through the process.

DISCUSSION

Looking back, our PSTs had, indeed, grown. From the start of the semester, we planned to assess, among other things, the development of their levels of reflection on education and themselves as teachers. In addition, we wanted to investigate how their perceptions about using artistic response strategies for their own learning and in their future teaching might change after being exposed to these strategies in a more deliberate way where teacher-pedagogy is discussed. To help measure their growth and perceptions, after completing the Photographic Philosophy, PSTs filled out a self-reflection. In addition, at the end of the semester, they took a final survey that asked about their experiences using artistic response strategies in this class and about their attitudes regarding using these strategies in their future teaching. We used these data to measure any change in student beliefs and attitudes in comparison to their first surveys.

In general, PSTs said that they were proud of their work and enjoyed the process of using the arts in combination with other strategies. Most PSTs said that these strategies, particularly the Photographic Philosophy, increased their learning.

In addition, every student said that they were more likely to use artistic strategies in their future classroom because they could see how these types of activities heightened students' motivation and would make their teaching more effective. One student stated, "I learned how to make assignments more interesting and engaging for students. I think this will make me a better teacher." PSTs also commented that using these strategies could increase students' ability to share their thinking and allow their peers to better critique their work, which they felt would benefit their students' learning.

In addition, many PSTs wrote that after consciously engaging with artistic analysis and composition they felt more comfortable applying these strategies in their future classrooms. One student wrote, "I think that I understand the concepts [of arts integration] better because now they aren't just words or concepts. Now, for example, when I think of the classroom community, which was the overall theme of our [Photographic Philosophy] ... it has a deeper meaning to me." Another student said, "I haven't had this done in a classroom yet and found it quite effective, so it really altered my views on ... how many different ways there are to teach and how I can teach in my own classroom."

CONCLUSION

Through my experience as a former high school ELA teacher, I came to the opinion that too often we as educators tell our students what is necessary and important rather than letting them experience it for themselves through creative exploration. When teachers allow students to explore in this way they encourage student buy-in, design lessons that students' value, and give students power over their learning. As education researcher, Steve Seidel (2012) writes:

Disconnecting seeing from making, as is the case so often in schools, reinforces a kind of passivity in students–their perception that the message of schooling is that you are supposed to take in what others have done but not create original work. The experience of being both a creator of valuable work as well as a critical, thoughtful audience for the work of others shifts the image of the student in his or her mind to one of an active contributor, highly engaged in the real work of a particular field, even if not quite yet at a professional level. (pp. 156–157)

As an ELA teacher educator, I have found the same to be true in my methods classroom—PSTs need to actively experience what they will teach, including using the arts as a way to think and learn. That is why I continue to bring this type of learning into my college-level methods courses. The Photographic Philosophy project, as discussed in this chapter, is just one example of the potential for using artistic strategies in methods courses. For PSTs, experiencing artistic methods is not the "fluff" of learning. It is part of the foundation. PSTs need to reposition themselves as able producers of artistic content in order to effectively use it in their pedagogy. It is essential for them to understand and trust the methods in order to be fully invested in their use in their future classrooms.

REFERENCES

Alsup, J. (2005). *Teacher identity discourses: Negotiating personal and professional spaces.* Routledge.

Beach, R., Campano, G., Edmiston, B., & Borgmann, M. (2010). *Literacy tools in the classroom: Teaching through a critical inquiry, grades 5–12.* Teachers College Press.

Britzman, D. P. (1992). "Is there a problem with knowing thyself? Toward a poststructuralist view of teacher identity." *Teacher Thinking, Teacher Knowing in Language and Literacy; Reflections on Literacy and Language Education 1992 Chicago, IL Conference,* National Council of Teachers of English.

Bulman, R. (2015). *Hollywood goes to high school: Cinema, schools, and American culture* (2nd ed.). Worth Publishers.

Chicola, N. A., & Smith, B. J. (2005). Integrating visual arts into instruction. *International Journal of Learning, 12*(1), 167–175.

Cohen, R. M., & Scheer, S. (Eds.). (1997). *The work of teachers in America: A social history through stories.* Routledge.

Connelly, M. F., & Clandinin, J. (1988). *Teachers as curriculum planners: Narratives of experience.* Teachers College Press.

Crick, R. D., & Grushka, K. (2009). Signs, symbols and metaphor: Linking self with text in inquiry-based learning. *The Curriculum Journal, 20*(4), 447–464.

Dalton, M. M. (2010). *The Hollywood curriculum: Teachers in the movies* (3rd ed.). Peter Lang.

Dunn, P. A. (2021). *Drawing conclusions: Using visual thinking to understand complex concepts in the classroom.* Teachers College Press.

Eisner, E. W., et al. (2010). *Literacy tools in the classroom: Teaching through critical inquiry, grades 5–12*. Teachers College Press.
Grant, A., Hutchinson, K., Hornsby, D., & Brooke, S. (2008). Creative pedagogies: "Artfull" reading and writing. *English Teaching: Practice and Critique, 7*(1), 57–72.
Harris, A. (2009). The good teacher: Images of teachers in popular culture. *English Drama Media, 14*, 11–18.
Hartman, P., Berg, J., Schuler, B., & Knauer, E. (2019). Using artistic response strategies meaningfully in the ELA classroom. In K. J. Macro & M. Zoss (Eds.), *A symphony of possibilities: A handbook for arts integration in secondary english language arts* (pp. 121–138). National Council of Teachers of English.
Hartman, P., Berg, J., Fulton, H., & Schuler, B. (2021). Memes as a means: Using popular culture to enhance character study. *Journal for Expanded Perspectives on Learning Journal, 26*, 66–82.
Heilman, R. (2001). The great-teacher myth. *The American Scholar, 60*(3), 417–423.
Holdren, T. S. (2012). Using art to access reading comprehension and critical thinking in adolescents. *Journal of Adolescent & Adult Literacy, 55*(8), 692–703.
Joseph, P. B., & Burnaford, G. (Eds.). (2001). *Images of schoolteachers in America* (2nd ed.). Routledge.
Knowles, J. G. (1992). Models of understanding pre-service and beginning teachers' biographies: Illustrations from case studies. In I. F. Goodison (Ed.), *Studying teachers' lives* (pp. 99–152). Routledge.
Labaree, D. F. (2000). On the nature of teaching and teacher education: Difficult practices that look easy. *Journal of Teacher Education, 51*(3), 228–233.
Liston, D. P., & Renga, I. (Eds.). (2014). *Teaching, learning, and schooling in film: Reel education*. Routledge.
Lortie, D. (2002). *Schoolteacher: A sociological study* (2nd ed.). University of Chicago Press.
Macro, K. J., & Zoss, M. (Eds.). (2019). *A symphony of possibilities: A handbook for arts integration in secondary English language arts*. National Council of Teachers of English.
Miller, S. R., & Hopper, P. F. (2010). Supporting reading goals through the visual arts. *Reading Improvement, 47*(1), 3–6.
Rosenblatt, L. M. (1978). *The reader, the text, the poem: The transactional theory of the literary work*. Southern Illinois University Press.
Seidel, S. (2012). "The only thing that will save us from ourselves": The arts, social engagement, and social transformation. In H. R. Kohl and T. Oppenheim (Eds.), *The muses go to school: Inspiring stories about the importance of arts in education* (pp. 147–163). New Press.
Shoffner, M. (Ed.). (2016). *Exploring teachers in fiction and film: Saviors, scapegoats, and schoolmarms*. Routledge.
Sidelnick, M. A., & Svoboda, M. L. (2000). The bridge between drawing and writing: Hannah's story. *The Reading Teacher, 54*(2), 174–184.
Weber, S. J., & Mitchell, C. (1995). *"That's funny you don't look like a teacher!": Interrogating images, identity, and popular culture*. Routledge.
Wilhelm, J. D. (2016). *"You gotta BE the book": Teaching engaged and reflective reading with adolescents* (2nd ed.). Teachers College Press.

CHAPTER 3

TAPESTRIES OF TEACHING

Flagging Philosophies of Education in Preservice Curriculum

Jeff Spanke

I'm still embarrassed to say that I never really gave the room much thought. I'd walked by the display hundreds of times over the years, and while certainly eye-catching, the roughly 160 international flags hanging from oak dowels at the west entrance of the student union's Great Hall had always seemed like more of a cool stop on a campus visit than a place where I would actually spend any meaningful time. My experience working with 55 teenagers from around the world, though, quickly shifted not only the way I viewed those flags and those dowels and those strangers sitting beneath them, but also how I would come to approach my role as an English teacher educator.

Each year, for the month of July, 45 different teenagers from 45 different European Union countries join ten American high school students as members of the Benjamin Franklin Transatlantic Fellowship (BFTF). Founded by the United States Department of State's Bureau of Education and Cultural Affair in 2006, the BFTF brings together a group of highly

---

Cultivating Democratic Literacy Through the Arts, pages 37–53
Copyright © 2024 by Information Age Publishing
www.infoagepub.com
All rights of reproduction in any form reserved.

recommended "fellows" from around the United States and Europe for an intensive, immersive program centered around diplomacy, international relations, media and journalism, and citizenship education.

Since 2015, I've had the pleasure of serving as an academic mentor, instructor, and Program Administrator for BFTF; in these capacities, I've worked with hundreds of brilliant, inquisitive minds from around the globe, learning with them, and sharing experiences that have helped cultivate our collective cultural, digital, and critical civic literacies (DeVitis, 2011). And interestingly enough, each year, regardless of the cohort, the institute always seems to kick off officially in the "Flag Room" of the student union.

It's our last stop on our Day One campus tour. As part of the institute's opening activities, after traveling for nearly an entire day, and while still very much fighting jetlag, my staff and I take our beleaguered fellows on a long walk around my alma mater, Purdue University, one of the hosts of the BFTF program. Without exception, the annual campus walking tour always culminates in the student union, where, after roughly an hour of basking in the hot July sun, our students find respite in the International Flag Display of the union's West Great Hall. The display features flags from every nation represented by a student at the university. The vibrant collection serves to acknowledge the international presence on campus, support the university's diversity initiatives, remind students of the value of study abroad opportunities, and represent the collegiate experience as one that prepares students for citizenship in today's global community. Each year, whenever we first enter the Flag Room, it never takes long for the tears to start shedding. And it's never from the Americans.

When the international fellows first enter the space, many immediately fall silent, their pacing nearly slowing to a halt. Almost in unison, their heads fall back, their eyes shooting toward the ceiling, frantically searching for their nation's woven emblem. When they find it, their faces beam, their lungs exhale, fingers start pointing, phones feebly capturing the site. Many start crying, perhaps out of fatigue from the journey that brought them so far from the only worlds they've ever known. For most of these kids, this is their first time outside the borders of their home countries, many of which are only a generation removed from Soviet control. These kids might not have seen liberation themselves; but their parents all did. And most of their grandparents never knew anything besides Communist occupation.

To these European ambassadors, their nations' flags bear a deeply personal significance to which their American counterparts just can't ever seem to relate. These flags *mean* something and reflect a consciousness with which these kids live every day; the preciousness, price, and fragility of democratic freedom.

Of course, the American fellows always echo their own respective love of country; and, of course, many have had family and friends serve in the

Armed Forces, or have otherwise made sacrifices in the name of the United States. But in their own ways, these Americans also, each year on Day One, realize that the ways other countries view their flags bear strikingly little semblance to the way they've always viewed theirs.

It was my experience with BFTF, and especially our time in Purdue's Flag Room, that compelled me to reevaluate what it means to be a member of a community; what it means to carry a flag and what it means to have that flag stand for something worth falling for. After years of serving the BFTF and its international fellows, I started considering ways in which I could marble the lessons of the Flag Room with my career as an English teacher educator. What could it look like to frame teacher preparation as a form of citizenship education in its own right? What might diplomacy mean in a curricular setting? How might the tenets of international relations apply to planning, instruction, and assessment? And finally, if Teaching, as a profession, can function as its own nation-of-sorts wherein Teachers are the citizens, what are the various conditions of membership? What flags do we weave? Which do we wave? How big are they, who carries them, and what values do they represent?

I offer this chapter as a means of composing this anthem further.

* * *

There is certainly no shortage of resources for how to craft a teaching philosophy. Nor is there a lack of scholarship that emphasizes the importance of developing a philosophy of education throughout teacher education programs. However, in my early years as an English teacher educator, I kept observing the same two issues with several of my preservice teachers.

The first issue involved the struggles that so many of them seemed to have with crafting a teaching philosophy for their student teaching applications. Even as they neared the end of their program, every semester it seemed that our upper-class students really had a hard time articulating their personal beliefs about education, and especially their respective roles as instruments of teaching and learning. While many could discuss, in broad, incontestable terms, their *ideas* about students or classrooms or schools, with few exceptions, when they needed to taxonomize those thoughts in the form of a structured system of personal values and principles, most of these students simply couldn't express themselves beyond the banality of platitudes.

The second issue I faced regarding my students' difficulty developing their philosophies of education involved the curious way in which so many of them seemed to frame "teaching" in the first place. Through their written artifacts and our class discussions, it appeared as though my students were conceiving of "teaching" as either a performative act or as the behavioral manifestation of an individual function, i.e., a teacher. In other words, my students were approaching "teaching" as something one *does* or something one *is*. Teaching was *not*, however, often couched as a *profession* with certain unique values, traditions, histories, agendas, or membership criteria. Nor were *teachers* discussed as professionals operating within the broader field of the Teaching Community. Teachers taught in schools, of course; but the schools themselves or the communities in which they operated had nothing to do with teaching. Rather, schools seemed to function as monoliths that existed homogeneously and independently of the teachers doing the teaching.

I suppose it stands to reason, then, that as my students neared the end of their program and began compiling their applications for student teaching and beyond, they struggled to position themselves as viable, holistic candidates for entry into a world that, prior to that point, had always been a simplified abstraction. They had been prepared to teach (as an act), and they had been taught to see themselves as teachers (as a function), but they had yet to operationalize the function and the action as an identity within the borders of the wider professional Discourse (Gee, 1990) of Teaching. They were citizens of no country; people with no citizenship.

In light of my students' tenuous courtship of their own teaching philosophies, and very much inspired by my experience working with the international fellows through BFTF, I decided to modify my "Introduction to English Language Arts" course to include a project that could help my preservice teachers develop a critical consciousness as "citizens" in the Teaching Community. More so than simply an exercise in crafting a philosophy of education, I knew that I wanted this new project to promote a sense of "critical civic literacy" (DeVitis, 2011) as it pertains to American public education. If Teaching, as a profession, functions along the same lines as other smaller communities or even larger nation-states, than citizenship or membership within Teaching demands a civically minded, democratic professional identity that must be cultivated throughout teacher preparation programs.

Just as a teacher's classroom may very well showcase difference aspects of their identities, I strove in this project for students to create artifacts that visually documented the *constitution*, of sorts, of their image of public education. *What is their philosophy of Teaching as a professional community? What does Teaching, to/for them, stand for, and how do they, as citizen-Teachers, operate within it? What comprises the fabrics of Teaching? What does its flag look like?* If the tapestries of their philosophies will one day hang from oak dowels in the entrance of some great hall, cramped together in a vibrant display of united (imagi)nations, who will walk in, look up, point out, and start crying? Who will say, "that's me, that one, right there, I'm that!"

Along these lines, I knew that I wanted the project to manifest as an aesthetically based "multimodal ensemble" (Serafini, 2015). In addition to articulating their Teaching philosophies in a traditional written form—akin to a nation's constitution—I wanted my students to design an artistic representation of their beliefs, values, and principles; a series of Teaching flags, as we grew to call them, that would visually signify the constitution of their unique Teaching communities in the same way that those hanging woven symbols signified over 160 nations to the fellows of BFTF.

But before we ever started weaving our Teaching flags, we first needed to determine what a flag actually *is* and how a single material item differs from a written list of important ideas. To that end, we needed to figure out how flags actually work and come to terms with the fact that even the strongest person in the world can only carry so many. This first task ultimately proved vital for the successful completion of this project.

WHAT MAKES A FLAG A FLAG

As we started considering the nature, design, and purpose of flags, my students and I developed our own operational criteria for the creation and utilization of flags. As Table 3.1 highlights, regardless of the size, shape, or source, all flags, we determined through much conversation and deliberation, share the following characteristics.

As my students and I continued framing flags both as metaphors of the Teaching Community and as emblematic of our identities of Teacher-citizens, the contestability and limitability of flags proved perhaps the most

TABLE 3.1 Characteristics of Flags

Visibility	Flags, by their nature, are meant to seen.
Functionality	Flags serve unique rhetorical purposes that distinguish them from other forms of signage.
Accessibility	The rhetoric function of flags needs to be accessible to, at the bare minimum, their intended audience; both the visual and rhetorical accessibility of flags demands a particular type of literacy.
Agreeability	Any flag is a function of consensus. A flag becomes a flag only after some group determines that the rhetorical function of the flag is appropriate and accessible and that the visual design serves the function's ends.
Tangibility	A flag is material thing; as such, its tangibility endows it with a certain preciousness and fragility that oftentimes accentuates its functionality while further distinguishing it from other banners, posters, or signs.
Malleability	Flags can be rendered into a variety of material forms without altering its accessibility or rhetorical function.
Contestability	All flags, by their nature, must stand in opposition to something else.
Limitability	All flags, as material artifacts, are inherently finite; all flags are also limited in terms of what they represent and how many can be carried at any one time, by any one person.

difficult yet important concepts to grasp. Through our navigation, we determined that a flag, by its nature, must stand in opposition to something else. An American flag is *not* a French flag, for example. Nor is an Australian flag a British flag. They may share similarities, both in terms of aesthetic design and rhetorical function—they may reflect the same values or principles and may be viewed just as preciously in their respective nations—but they are inherently *not* the same thing.

The distinction between flags may be more subtle and amicable, or polarizing and oppositional. A flag may elicit anger and revolt or precipitate feelings of hatred or oppression. But even the most peaceful and aesthetically pleasing flags, representing the most humane and loving of principles, can never encapsulate the entirety of humanity. My BFTF fellows never seemed to care that their flags were opposed by the flags of other nations (Russia and Ukraine, for instance); but in the initial stages of the Flags Assignment, my preservice teachers really seemed to struggle with the idea that their values might contradict the ideas of others. Clearly, the contestability of flags was something we needed to reconcile.

Along these lines, throughout our discussions, my students and I determined that the limitability of flags exists on two levels. The first speaks to the extent to which any flag, because of its tangible nature, cannot last forever. Their finitude stems from the fragility of their material construction. Flags rip, tear, burn, or fade. Their fabrics may stain easily or fray over time with enough added stress. If nothing else, their structural integrity ultimately weakens with age, and while flags can be mended, their susceptibility to various elements means that their capacity to withstand the tests of time is limited from the start. Even the strongest flags eventually break down. And when they inevitably do, we face a choice; do we simply make more flags, in the same image as before, or do we change the design in accordance with the evolution of our (imagi)nation?

As my students and I concluded, flags are also limited in terms of the amount that can be carried or waved at any one time, by any one person. Flags have mass. They can be heavy and awkward to maneuver. They can be cumbersome to wave and difficult to transport, depending on their size. Even when folded or rolled, a single person can only handle so many flags at once. In the same vein that a flag's contestability proved a difficult concept for my students to grasp, the inability to carry an infinite number of inherently finite flags seemed to confound my students' wishes to be a staunch advocate for every conceivable cause. Despite the contemporary negative connotations of the term, once we accepted that we can only carry so many flags as Teachers, we realized we needed to *discriminate*. Make decisions. Take stances. But we also knew that just because we might not necessarily be able to carry *all of the flags*, that doesn't mean we don't support the causes for which those flags fly; it only means that we can only bear the weight of so much with the little we have. And with that, we had laid the foundation for the creation of our new united (imagi)nations.

THE FLAGS ASSIGNMENT

Even though I also taught upper-level ELA methods courses and supervised our student teachers, I decided to include this new Flags Assignment as the capstone project for ENG 150: Introduction to English Language Arts. At the time, I was Assistant Professor of English Education at a midsized, Midwestern university and had been teaching ENG 150 for a few years. Students in our program usually take this course during their first semester. As an entry point into the teaching profession, the course offers students a variety of ideas, approaches, scholarship, and onsite, practical experiences related, broadly, to the teaching of English Language Arts. What better way, I thought, to conclude this pivotal emergence into the Teaching Community than to have students design a collection of flags that represents and reflects how they each conceive of our field's constitution?

We designed the project as a class, beginning first by generating a list of governing questions or critical inquiries that sought to guide us in our philosophical "weaving." Based on these questions, we decided that students would construct and compile a collection of flags, each of which would highlight one unique principle/value/belief they have with regard to a holistic view of Teaching, (i.e., as profession, action, function, identity). The specific design and form of the flags could vary, but each flag needed to represent one element of my students' philosophy of Teaching-as-Community, and/or their roles as Teacher-citizens therein. To help facilitate their thinking, we generated the following questions:

- What specific issues/ideas/values are important to me as a teacher?
- What do I consider myself a master of/over?
- What curricular theories or movements do I espouse? Which do I oppose?
- What am I willing to fall for? To fight for? To stand for?
- With what philosophies or pedagogies do I wish to align myself?
- What do I want to be "known for" within my school community?
- How will I decorate my room? What will it say about me?
- What will constitute my teacher identity?
- What knowledge is of most worth?
- What will my "thank you note" say?

Having curated our list of essential questions—which, by extension, served as our learning objectives or central focus for this project—we then began considering just how many flags we should make in order to satisfy the expectations of this project. Did the number really matter? Did the size? How many is too many, how many too few? What about the form? Do the flags need to be cloth? Some other fabric? Do they even need to be tangible at all? What evaluation criteria do we even have here; by what metric are we assessing success, and what learning objectives does this project meet? How we do grade art, anyway, and what does that grade actually mean?

I should note that we started having these conversations within the first few weeks of the semester. Even though the project wouldn't be due until the end of the term, I wanted to model to my students the principles of backward/universal design. In this case, we start with the learning objectives, manifested as the critical inquiries we generated as a class. Once we've established our objectives—the *point*, the "so what?"—we figure out how we're going to measure them. If, in real life, I find myself hungry, my goal becomes to somehow get some food. But of course I don't just get in the car and start driving. I first should probably figure out where I want to go and how I'll know if that place will give me what I need. If I'm hungry, I go get food; I don't go buy batteries.

I wanted my students to learn, in other words, that Teaching doesn't just start whenever we step in front of students. Nor, as Teachers, do we just sit down and aimlessly start making lesson plans. Teachers first need to figure out what they're going to teach before they ever put pen to paper or fingers to keys. We need to know we're hungry before we start eating.

The second step is determining how we're going to know if we taught the thing we wanted to teach. How will we measure our success, how will we know if we're full? Only then can we determine how we're going to satisfy our hunger. We usually don't turn the car on until we figure out where we're going (our objective) and why we're going there (our assessment).

As a way of modeling/exploring the principles of curricular design and assessment creation, my students and I came to the consensus that, unless we're actually going to be learning how to create art—i.e., paint, weave, draw, etc.—we're really not in a position to evaluate the quality of the art— the flags—themselves. As Teachers, we can only assess either what we taught or what we somehow determined our students already know. Assessments must align with objectives, in other words, and since this wasn't an art class, their grades on this assignment must derive from something other than the aesthetic "merit" of their final creations.

To satisfy this curricular demand, we determined that these projects should be evaluated based on three distinct elements, each weighted separately and each containing their own assessment criteria. Table 3.2 highlights an abbreviated rubric that my students and I created for the Flags assignment.

As the rubric demonstrates, my students thought it was important that the project be evaluated based on a variety of elements. For instance, we

TABLE 3.2 Flags Assignment Rubric

Element	Project Percentage	Evaluation Criteria	
Flag creation	10%	1. Did you create a multimodal, arts-based *collection* of flags?	Yes = 5%, No = 0%
		2. Does each flag visually represent a unique philosophy/value/principle pertaining to education?	Yes = 5%, No = 0%
Flag presentation	30%	1. Did you present on your assigned day?	Yes = 5%, No = 0%
		2. Did you present in the allotted time?	Yes = 5%, No = 0%
		3. Did you explain the rhetorical function of *each* flag?	Yes = 5%, No = 0%
		4. Did you connect each flag to research/scholarship?	Yes = 5%, No = 0%
		5. Did you discuss the affordances and limitations of each flag?	Yes = 5%, No = 0%
		6. Could you physically carry all of your flags by yourself?	Yes = 5%, No = 0%
Flag explication	60%	• See "Artist's Statement" Rubric[a]	

[a] a more comprehensive set of evaluation criteria was distributed separately for this written component.

determined that I would evaluate forty percent of the project based on my students' creation and presentation of the flags themselves. The points that students earned on these components would derive solely from completion, with no gradation between earning full credit on the respective elements and earning zero credit. The students either presented their work, or not. Either they made the flags, or they didn't.

The bulk of the points earned on this assignment came from a traditional written composition which we collectively called an "Artist's Statement." For this element, students performed a much more intellectually robust explication of their artwork, marbling their creations with credible research, personal experiences, critical reflection, and scholarly analysis. The flags were what people might see in the museum, we decided; the artist's statement is what they would read in the program about the artistic pieces and the various cognitive and aesthetic processes that contributed to their generation. As a triangulated metric, the flags, the presentation, and the artist's statement comprised the summative assessment of the flags assignment.

With our objectives defined and our evaluation criteria set, my students and I wrapped up Week 3 of the semester and prepared ourselves to spend the reminder of our time together learning the skills, forming the insights, and developing the critical habits of mind needed to complete our arts-based flags project. Roughly twelve weeks later, my students and I gathered in our classroom yet again, this time fully prepared to start showcasing the fruits of our collective cognitive and creative labors.

THE PRESENTATION OF FLAGS, A CEREMONY OF SORTS

I confess that I never expected the flag presentations in ENG 150 to mirror so profoundly the experience of walking into the International Flag Display with the BFTF fellows. But in many ways, the two distinct experiences were actually quite similar. For starters, my students and I were instantly taken aback by the sheer vibrancy of the literally dozens of flags that my nineteen students brought with them to class on the first day of presentations. The colors and textures, symbols and words all immediately coated our space like swatches on an easel. Because we had no set parameters for the specific material of the flags, the colorful cornucopia of student creations truly ran the gamut from painted canvases and photocollages, to needlepoint work and digital designs printed on foam posterboard.

Some students strolled in carrying only a few flags; others nearly tripped over the several rolled pieces awkwardly protruding from their pockets and bags. Some clearly spend hours crafting two or three larger, more intricate flags, while others spent perhaps equal time making several, more simplified, smaller flags. Some flags were filled with words and phrases, others only with images or drawings. Some were neat and polished, others messy and obscure. Yet without exception, much like the fellows standing beneath their nation's flag in the student union, each of my students showed up on Presentation Day with a unique and, in several cases, a previously unseen sense of stake and conviction.

Their presentations further highlighted the complexities and nuances of the flags assignment which, as the final weeks of the semester unfolded, had successfully evolved into a viable metaphor for philosophies of education and for viewing Teaching not only as a function or action, but also as a unique professional community/identity in its own right.

"I knew that I really wanted to have a lot of flags," one student noted in her presentation. "I have lots of things that I believe in and stand for. But it got hard to literally carry them all at once, so I had to make them smaller and couldn't spend as much time on any of them as I wanted. Some of them aren't really done yet."

Another student explained that he'd "rather have a few, really strong values and principles that I could develop and turn into something really cool and powerful instead of lots of little things that distract me and take my attention from other things." Other students followed suit, noting specifically the unanticipated difficulties in actually making a flag that represented something they believed in. "It's easy to, like, *say* you stand for something," one girl explained:

> But when we had to actually figure out what it looks like in a way that wasn't just writing it in some essay, and then also figure out a way to get it to class, it got a lot harder. You also never know what people are gonna think when they see your flags, and that can really start to mess with you, too.

As more and more students expressed their initial anxieties with manifesting their philosophies in an arts-based flag form, the metaphor seemed to grow more applicable to how these students were starting to conceive of themselves as Teachers within the broader Teaching Community. "I mean, like, I really value *inclusion*," one student said during their presentation:

> But *my* idea of inclusion is different than somebody else's, right? So, like, what does my idea look like? What makes my idea of inclusion special or different? And how can I make that into something visible? I can't just say I value inclusion. I had to show it, and that was really challenging. But also fun.

Along these lines, aside from the difficulties my students had determining the logistics of their flags—size, design, number, form, etc.—the act of presenting them to the class made for a more compelling element to the project than it seemed any of us had originally anticipated. A certain vulnerability quickly seemed to eclipse the sense of pride and ownership that initially governed the space. It was one thing for my students to make their own flags and bring them to class; it soon became another matter for them to explain—and by extension, *defend*—their beliefs to their peers. Here, the inherent contestability of flags—and, more broadly, all philosophies—rose to the forefront.

"I was really proud of my [pop culture] flag," one student said. "I love pop culture, and I really think that it's going to be a big part of my teacher identity. But, like, nobody else here seems to think it's a good idea at all, and I'm now I'm really nervous that I screwed this up." Upon hearing this, several of this student's peers expressed support for his views on pop culture, explaining that they loved pop culture, too, and that the student didn't do anything wrong at all. And of course these students are right.

But this unprompted dialogue sparked another insight into this experience. The student who valued pop culture couched that passion in a contingency that was based on the approval of his peers. Because they didn't visibly echo his love of pop culture in their flags, he convinced himself that he had made some sort of mistake, as if philosophies and values, at some level, need to be absolute or universal. Adding to this anxiety, because his peers didn't also create flags for pop culture, he was also convinced that they didn't value it. Our ensuing conversation revealed that both of these assumptions are flawed.

No, my students and I discussed, as Teachers, not everyone will carry the same identical flags. Not only will our flags look different and function differently and be created with varying degrees of sacrifice, investment, and reflection—different flags have different stakes—but they will also, more often than not in some cases, be the only ones of their type flying in our communities. But that doesn't mean we should take them down. And it doesn't mean that our fellow Teachers don't also agree with us or share the same principles; it only means that they have their own flags and only so many ways—or so much energy—to carry them.

Still, despite the apparent efficacy of having students create and present artistic representations of their Teaching philosophies, especially in terms of what these exercises reveal about how my students were positioning themselves within the broader Teaching Community, it was their written reflections—their Artist Statements—that truly seemed to distinguish the Flags Assignment from other, more traditional ways of composing philosophies of education.

THE ARTIST STATEMENTS

Just as the flag presentations showcased a variety of tensions and apprehensions that neither my students nor I anticipated in terms of how they conceived of and negotiated their respective principles and values of education, their written compositions demonstrated that the artistic process of developing their beliefs in aesthetic, tangible forms ultimately helped them each cultivate stronger, more precise positionalities and dispositions as Teachers in the Teaching Community.

"When I first started thinking about what I believed in about teaching," one student wrote:

> My ideas all seemed pretty good but also really broad. They were safe because nobody could disagree with anything I was saying, which probably meant that they weren't the strongest they could be. But when I started figuring out ways to make these beliefs into actual flags, I realized that I needed to be more specific with what I was meaning. And that really helped, I think.

Other students mirrored these sentiments in their artist statements, noting specifically how their beliefs evolved and solidified in response to the aesthetic, material demands of the project. The deliberation and artistic considerations that, by design, went into creating the flags seemed to have the ancillary benefit of compelling these students to make critically reflective decisions about the nuanced nature of their values in ways that other forms of composition might not have required.

"I've written other philosophies of education for other classes before," one student commented in his essay:

> And those were always just really vague and simple... I think it helped knowing that my peers would be seeing our flags, that it wasn't just the instructor. Knowing that I'd have to defend them in class also made me pay more attention to what they looked like, what they meant, and what they said about me. It was different than just writing them down.

Of the nineteen students enrolled in my class, sixteen wrote specifically about how their Teaching philosophies evolved through the process of creating their Teaching flags. Table 3.3 provides a snapshot of these evolutions, based on these sixteen students' Artist Statements.

As Table 3.3 highlights, through using an arts-based approach in the creation and articulation of philosophies of education, my students were not only able to ground their respective pedagogical constitutions in research-based, scholarly discourses, but in doing so, they were also laying the ground work for their own potential marketability and community membership. "I'm pretty sure all teachers are passionate about *something*," one student commented in her artist statement:

> So it wasn't enough for me to just say that I value passion in my teaching. But when I started making my Passion Flag, I really started to think about what, specifically, I was passionate about, and I kept coming back to queer theory and fashion studies... And I really think the fact that I can say this *now* will really help me on the job market.

Likewise, her peers expressed similar ideas. Several students, for example, wrote that they wanted their classrooms to serve as "safe spaces" for their

TABLE 3.3 The Evolution of Students' Teaching Philosophies Through Creating Teaching Flags

Students' Values Before Creating Flags	Themes of Flags Created by Students
Passion	Queer Theory/Fashion Studies
Reading	Historical Fiction/Creative Non-Fiction
Writing	Flash/Fan Fiction
Discussions	Interdisciplinarity/Collaboration
Creativity	Arts-based Pedagogy
Curiosity	Critical Inquiry/Community Activism
Safe Space	Mental Health Stigma/Young Adult Lit
Fun	Digital Citizenship/Media Literacy
Discovery	Immersive/Problem-Based Learning
History	Early 20th Century American Blackness

students; but in each of their respective flags, the idea of "safe space" manifested in different ways, each speaking to particular aspects of their creators' personalities and dispositions. In other words, the artistic demands of the Flags Assignment resulted in much more refined and deliberate displays of my students' philosophies of education than a traditional written document likely would have generated.

As my students and I grew to understand over the course of our semester's waning weeks, the arts-based process of designing flags that were unique to their identities and positionalities as members of the Teaching Community ultimately resulted in their symbolic emergence into a world bigger than themselves. The flags became not just individual identity markers, but relational, and in very much the same way that my fellows' national flags ultimately linked them to (but also distinguished them from) the other members of the BFTF cohort, my students grew to realize that their Teaching flags became not only synonymous with them as Teacher-citizens, but also with their inclusion in the broader Teaching Community.

The triangulation of the flags themselves, the oral presentation, and the written explication offers valuable insight into the viability of imbuing arts-based experiences into preservice education courses, particularly with regard to their efficacy in helping future educators develop their teaching philosophies.

UNITED (IMAGI)NATIONS: THE LESSONS OF THE FLAGS ASSIGNMENT

Like the flags of many nations around the world, the final summative assignment of ENG 150 has evolved since its inception. Over the years, I've experimented with different forms and functions of the flags, as well as with the various parameters and policies of the presentations. But the core of the project has always remained the same; it is unequivocally an arts-based endeavor. Despite fluctuations to specific elements of the experience, I have never wavered from perhaps my most dominant flag that arts-based experiences belong alongside ELA instruction.

In the case of my ENG 150 Flags Assignment, the inclusion of artistic modes of expression consistently results in much more than my students' ability to write a teaching philosophy. Regardless of the semester, the Flags Assignment has contributed to my students' personal and professional growth in the following areas.

Teaching as Community

The artistic component to the Flags Assignment ignites my students' imaginations, not only in terms how to bring their beliefs and principles to life, but also how those tenets contribute to their broader conceptions of Teaching as Community. Similar to how the American Constitution served as the Founding Fathers' blueprint for a nation that didn't yet exist, my students' flags—as material manifestations of their values—serve to chart their course of a world they'll one day have their hands in creating. The flags allow my students to tether their beliefs to something beyond their personal grasp, a professional community with various borders and boundaries, privileges and power structures. Their flags demand a confrontation of the excluded and marginalized, the oppressed and the proverbial "Not Pictured." As my students make and carry their flags, they're forced to come to terms with everything they *didn't* make or *can't* carry. Or simply rejected or dismissed. As my students begin visualizing the communities that their flags represent, they start reconciling the inevitable complexities of those communities and how their initial constitutions might very well conflict with other aspects of their chosen profession. Such is the case, we learn, with all communities.

Teacher as Citizen

As visual metaphors for my students' philosophies of education, their Teaching flags also reflect the conditions of citizenship within an external community. Each flag my students create represents both the rights and responsibilities that they feel they bring to the profession. Just as the creation of the flags demands the cultivation of particular habits of mind, the flags themselves signify the habits of mind that my students deem necessary for citizenship in Teaching. As flags, my students beliefs about education no longer exist as detached or mercurial aspirations, but rather as more solidified constructs that inform and underscore their emergence into a world outside their own heads. The flags transform these students from being people with thoughts to professionals with purposes. In that sense, through constructing their own flags, my students start accepting the responsibility and fragility of the values that those flags depict, as well as their complex roles in the preservation and perpetuation of those principles.

Teaching as Civic Contribution

Perhaps the greatest lesson to be learned from the infusion of art in the creation of teaching philosophies is the sense of stake and investment it promotes in students. In ways that traditional compositions simply can't capture, these flags taught my students that as Teacher-citizens within the Teaching Community, their primary duty is to their fellow citizens within their communities. In this sense, the Flags Assignment instilled in my preservice teachers a spirit of community activism and civic engagement, propelling their professional development and dramatically bolstering their community investment. When they started seeing themselves as agentic, holistic professionals within an established, well-constituted Teaching Community, they started embracing the accountability and responsibilities that these roles necessitated. In short, as opposed to vague insights or banal platitudes, my students had each now woven something that suggested that, at some level, they had something to offer the field. They had something to get up for and contribute. Something to fall for and wave on the frontlines; finally, something to stand under, aspire toward, look to, point out, and start crying, "that's me, that one, right there, I'm that!"

CONCLUSION

On Christmas Eve, 2022, the pipes in my campus building burst in the night. The ensuing flood was so devastating, and the temperatures that caused it were so low, that within minutes water started leaking from the outside wall of the brick building, freezing in midair and resulting in a scene that looked simultaneously like beautiful two-story frozen waterfalls and thousands of dollars' worth of property damage.

For the most part, my second floor office was spared, but everything I had stored over the years in boxes on the floor was destroyed. Copies of old syllabi and student papers; spiralbound coursepacks from graduate school that I'd saved from an age before everything was put online; handwritten field notes from my dissertation research; and four repurposed imported beer boxes overstuffed with virtually every flag my ENG 150 students have ever made.

Since first arriving at my university in 2016, it didn't take long for the walls of my office to be adorned with class artifacts and other student projects. Yes, many of those early canvases and cloths came from the Flags Assignment, but for the most part, I had saved all of the flags in cardboard boxes beneath my packed bookshelves. When I returned to campus in early January, 2023, I discovered that all of those boxes had been thrown away sometime over winter break: The risk of mold was too high, we were told.

I thought of the Flags Room and my European fellows; of the pride they always beam when seeing their nations' flags and of the horror they'd feel if the room itself suddenly burst into flames or got soaked from burst pipes. The tears would once again flow, for sure.

But even though the BFTF fellows often become synonymous with their countries over the course of the program, to the point where we often literally refer to each other by where we're from—*Hey, Moldova! What's up, Belarus?*—everyone knows that we're always more than whatever symbols represent us.

As I rang in the New Year by standing in the doorway of my flooded office, inhaling the dampness of musty tiles and trying to drown out the humming of industrial fans, I realized that what always made the Flags Assignment successful wasn't that my students somehow enshrined their beliefs in a precious multimodal artifact; it's that they used art to explore and defend how they themselves are already precious. *They* are the shrines, not their flags.

They don't need a flag in their window to be an ally for their students, and taking away our poles doesn't mean we can't fly our flags in ways our opposition cannot see. Flags burn, pipes burst, and buildings flood. But through using art to interrogate their own constitutions, my students learned that the strength of any flag lies not in its construction, but in the integrity of those who made and defend it. As Teacher-citizens in the Teaching Community, my students learned that the flags they made, while finite in themselves, always represented a set of dispositions of habits of mind that no canvas, fabric, or frame can ever contain. And I guess in that sense, no fire or flood can ever really destroy them.

Nevertheless, as we also learn, the Teaching Community is rife with pipes that burst and floods that flow freely through the halls of our united (imagi)nations. Yes, any Teacher-citizen is more than their flags—but that doesn't mean we shouldn't also have some plastic containers and shelves for storage, just in case the floors get messy.

REFERENCES

DeVitis, J. L. (2011). *Critical civic literacy: A reader.* Peter Lang.

Gee, J. P. (1990). Literacy, discourse, and linguistics: An introduction, *The Journal of Education, 171*(1), 5–176.

Serafini, F. (2015). Multimodal literacy: From theory to practice, *Language Arts, 92*(6), 412–423.

CHAPTER 4

USING VISUAL STORYTELLING TO SUPPORT DEMOCRATIC APPROACHES TO LITERACY INSTRUCTION

Wendy R. Williams

Using visual storytelling in English education can be an excellent way to support democratic approaches to literacy instruction. Visual forms such as comics, graphic novels, and zines (i.e., small, self-published booklets) can immerse readers into a character's or writer's culture and experiences, promoting empathy. They can also be used to call out injustices and advocate for change. Visual narratives can be highly engaging for readers of all levels, and they can stand as masterful works of art in their own right. Fortunately for teachers and students, under the large umbrella of young adult (YA) literature are many graphic novels and illustrated books to choose from. Students can also share stories of their own through these artistic forms. Along the way, teachers can help students cultivate the visual literacy skills they will need to effectively communicate with images.

In this chapter, I consider visual storytelling's potential for supporting democratic approaches to literacy learning. I explore some of the ways that comics, graphic novels, and zines have been used in education, provide an overview of how I used visual storytelling in my YA literature course, and share findings from a qualitative case study of three students. The chapter closes with some implications for teaching.

VISUAL LITERACY

Students need to develop visual literacy in order to communicate effectively in today's world and be prepared for the changing demands of college and careers (Council of Writing Program Administrators, et al., 2011). Preservice teachers in particular need experiences analyzing and composing visual narratives so they understand how different visual elements communicate meaning in graphic novels, comics, picturebooks, films, animation, and other visual forms of storytelling.

In my past teaching and research, I have found that teachers can support students in building visual literacy through a three-step process: focused study of visual elements, analysis of visual narratives, and creation of original visual narratives (Williams, 2019). In my university-level teaching, students have analyzed and composed visual works such as picturebooks, graphic novels, stop-motion animation, traditional animation, short films, movies, commercials, music videos, and videogames. It is worth mentioning that I do not expect students to walk into my English courses as accomplished visual artists. Skills and literacies—whether we are talking about writing or making art—are developed over time and with practice. We must therefore apply the same patience to the teaching of visual literacy that we apply to the teaching of linguistic literacy. Students are at different levels, but they can expand their skills with instruction, models, practice, and feedback.

COMICS, GRAPHIC NOVELS, AND ZINES

Visual storytelling forms, such as comics and graphic novels, have been used in education in a variety of ways, including to "illustrate points about gender, history, sociology, philosophy, mathematics, and even medicine" (Weiner & Syma, 2013, p. 1). Comics and graphic novels have effectively been used at the college level "to explore personal identity and cultural narratives" (Marrall, 2013, p. 245). Research has shown that English language learners can benefit from reading visual narratives, building their language skills and critical literacy through their encounters with these texts (Park, 2016). Graphic novels "blend...art, literature, and culture" and have wonderful potential for teaching visual literacy (Kwon, 2020, p. 34). Students might compose graphic novellas, review graphic novels visually, or summarize a graphic novel in the style of that book (Kwon, 2020). Such assignments have potential as "socially engaged education resources" (p. 39). Having students make their own visual narratives can support their writing skills, invite them to think creatively, connect them to authentic audiences, and spark interest and enjoyment related to the act of writing (Maliszewski, 2013).

Zines are a visual form that may be less familiar to students. These "self-published magazines...combine images, text, writing, photography, and/or poetry" (Klein, 2010, p. 40). The word "comes from...*fanzine*, a term coined in the 1930s to refer to self-publication of readers' reactions to comic books and science fiction publications" (Guzzetti & Gamboa, 2004, p. 408). Klein (2010) has used zines with pre-service teachers to support "storytelling, self-expression, teacher identity construction, and collaboration" (p. 42). In her course, students are asked to make one-page zines that share an "important, eye-opening, puzzling, disturbing, or humorous event/incident observed in a K–12 art classroom over the course of a semester" (p. 42), and these projects become "a mechanism to critically examine beliefs, assumptions, and concerns about art teaching" (p. 44). There is some disagreement over whether teachers should assign zines in formal educational settings (Guzzetti & Gamboa, 2004); however, my own opinion is that students should learn about zines and other visual forms, so they feel comfortable reading and writing regardless of the shape a work takes.

Comic and zine assignments deserve a place in teacher education programs because they give pre-service teachers practice communicating through visual and linguistic modes and help them develop a deeper appreciation for stories with images. This knowledge will serve them well as they go on to teach graphic novels, novels containing zines, illustrated books, and other forms of visual narrative. Teaching reading and writing is more complicated than ever because students need to be able to communicate through a variety of modes, such as linguistic, visual, audio, gestural, and spatial (New London Group, 1996).

COURSE OVERVIEW

At Arizona State University, I teach an upper-division undergraduate ENG 471 Literature for Young Adults course that is required for pre-service teachers. My course goals are for students to become familiar with a wide array of YA literature and respond to these works through different types of assignments that they could use with secondary students. I believe that making literacy learning more democratic for all students requires that teachers design inclusive curriculum, provide students with choice, and craft assignments that invite different kinds of expression.

During the spring 2021 semester, I taught one section of ENG 471 Literature for Young Adults in an online, asynchronous seven-week format. In an asynchronous course, the work for each week is posted in advance, and students go in and complete it by the deadline. The students may never meet the instructor or each other. I have taught many courses in this format for years, and it requires different instructional design than a face-to-face or synchronous online course. I have found it helps to keep deadlines the same each week (e.g., Sundays at 11:59 p.m.) and have a similar pattern of assignments due (e.g., two pieces per week). In a seven-week course, things move extremely quickly, so directions must be very clear. Scaffolding in this sort of teaching environment involves curating the materials students will need to complete an assignment and arranging these items in an order that moves students through logical steps. Course planning also involves thinking across the larger structure of the course. For example, weeks two and four in this course were designed to help students expand their visual literacy.

In week two, students were introduced to the concept of visual literacy through several short, high-interest videos:

- Brian Kennedy's "Visual Literacy" (https://www.youtube.com/watch?v=O39niAzuapc)
- "George Lucas: Teaching 'Communication'" (https://www.youtube.com/watch?v=GwDXlA_6usI&t=2s)
- "Martin Scorsese on the Importance of Visual Literacy" (https://www.youtube.com/watch?v=I90ZluYvHic&t=2s)
- Gene Luen Yang's "Comics Belong in the Classroom" (https://www.ted.com/talks/gene_luen_yang_comics_belong_in_the_classroom?language=en#t-288607)

Then students read one of three YA books with visuals: *Trickster: Native American Tales* (Dembicki, 2010), *Anya's Ghost* (Brosgol, 2011), or *The Invention of Hugo Cabret* (Selznick, 2007). For background on visual elements and how these elements communicate meaning, students read Frank Serafini's (2014) chapter, "The Elements of Art, Design, and Visual Composition." A 750-word visual analysis of their chosen book was due at the end of this week, which meant that students would need to photograph three pages from their book and apply three concepts from Serafini's (2014) chapter to each of these images. Since visual analysis writing is new for most students, I provided a "How to Write a Visual Analysis" guide with a sample body paragraph. I also posted an assignment rubric. Grading focused on the use of visual elements and evidence in the paper (i.e., terms explained using the provided chapter, specific examples from the YA book, photographs included, material cited correctly) and the quality of the writing (i.e., organization, voice, style, conventions).

In week four, students read another book with visuals from this list: *Gabi, A Girl in Pieces* (Quintero, 2014), *American Born Chinese* (Yang, 2006), or *The First Rule of Punk* (Perez, 2017). These texts functioned as mentor texts that students could look back to as they composed their own zine or comic, due at the end of the week. Students had access to a variety of materials about zines and comics, so they could learn more about these forms:

- "How To: Zines" (https://www.youtube.com/watch?v=C6cUie23VII)
- "Make a Foldy Zine" (http://zineopolis.blogspot.com/p/h.html)
- *Understanding Comics* (McCloud, 1993) excerpt
- *Making Comics* (McCloud, 2006) excerpt
- *How to Draw Comics the Marvel Way* (Lee & Buscema, 1978) excerpt

For the comic/zine project, students were asked to make six panels (for comics) or six pages (for zines) that told a story. These projects could share a personal experience or something from their culture. Along with the project, a 300-word artist statement was due. These statements needed to include a summary of the story, identify at least five visual elements used in the project, describe the process and tools used, and share their ideas about using projects like these in the secondary classroom. The rubric for this project focused on completeness of the work (i.e., at least six pages/panels sharing a story, an artist statement containing all required components) and effort shown (i.e., detail, color, legible text).

STUDY DESIGN

This qualitative study involved students from Arizona State University, which is one of the largest universities in the United States and an institution with a long history of online education. The study took place immediately after my online spring ENG 471 Literature for Young Adults course ended in spring 2021. Two research questions guided this work:

1. What visual elements do students use to make sense of YA visual narratives?
2. What visual elements do they use in their own comic/zine projects?

Using IRB-approved consent forms, I invited all 23 students in the course to participate in the study, and nine students joined. This chapter presents case studies of three of these participants: Taylor, Li, and Angelina. I downloaded their visual analysis papers and comic/zine projects (including artist statements) from Canvas. Also, two of these three participants took part in an optional 10-item structured interview. As the pandemic was in full swing, participants had the option to type responses to each question and email them to me or participate in an interview over Zoom. I loaded these research documents into NVivo, a data management program, and coded according to the visual elements used. I present these findings below.

THREE CASES

Taylor

Taylor (they/them) is a 19-year-old white, non-binary student whose interests include reading, writing, art, playing and coaching volleyball, and watching shows. When reflecting on this YA course, one of the books this student spoke about was the graphic novel, *They Called Us Enemy* (Takei, et al., 2019), valuing the book for its cultural importance and beautiful artwork, which pulls readers into the story.

In week two, reading Serafini's (2014) chapter helped Taylor notice how visual elements were at work in the graphic novel *Anya's Ghost* (Brosgol, 2011). In their visual analysis paper, this student wrote about the use of dot, line, shape, orientation, narrative structure, information zones, color, borders, and contact-gaze in the book. To illustrate, Taylor quoted from Serafini's (2014) chapter about how darker colors can be "scary" and "depressing" (p. 58) and explained that in the story, "the coloring of page 15 is markedly different than the others, still having bluish-purple hues but focusing more on blacks and greys." This change in color conveys "not only a shift in setting but also a foreshadowing of what Anya would find in the well after falling." Taylor observed that "there is not a single panel without intention" in this book.

In our interview conducted over Zoom, Taylor said that studying visual elements helped them read in a more focused way and that this knowledge is useful for students to have:

> We were reading [chapter 5 from Frank Serafini's book] and I [noticed] the importance of how this panel [in *Anya's Ghost*] is slanted toward the bottom and how this one has more blue colors than warm colors. It made me have a deeper appreciation for graphic novels and manga.... I think it's important for kids growing up to have [this training].

Using Visual Storytelling to Support Democratic Approaches to Literacy Instruction • **61**

Taylor also expressed that a lot of thought goes into just one panel of a comic, as artists must consider a variety of visual elements such as lighting and color.

In week four, Taylor applied this knowledge of visual concepts by making an original comic, "Pierogi" (see Figure 4.1). This student explained that "the six panels follow a young girl walking through a school hallway to

Figure 4.1 Pierogi comic.

lunch. She sees that her mother packed her pierogi for lunch and immediately imagines the horrific taunting she will endure. She goes to the girls' bathroom...and proceeds to flush her pierogi down the toilet." To construct this comic, Taylor used a sketchpad, pencil, pen, and markers. After sketching out all of the panels, the student colored and inked the comic. In the artist statement, Taylor reflected on having considered the use of color, dot, line, size/scale, and typography. For example:

- **Color**: I chose more cool tones, like mauve and purple and grey to produce a cooler atmosphere.
- **Dot**: I put dots on the pierogi to draw attention to them, forcing a focal point in the panels.
- **Size/Scale**: I made the second panel the largest one because I felt it was the most important...It represents the turning point in the panels and thus needed more attention.

Taylor came to this course already having an appreciation for graphic novels and manga, but now this student also sees the need to "advocate for more inclusion of graphic novels" in education. Taylor is looking forward to using visual works in the classroom to help students learn about different cultures and perspectives and to make reading more accessible to students. In other words, they see the potential of using visual storytelling to make education more democratic.

Li

Li (she/her) is a 21-year-old Chinese and Thai female who enjoys reading, cooking, and hiking. This student said that reading *The First Rule of Punk* (Pérez, 2017) was especially meaningful for her, given her mixed heritage. This book intersperses zines into the narrative.

In her visual analysis paper, which examined *The Invention of Hugo Cabret* (Selznick, 2007), Li wrote about information zones, lines, color, size/scale, salience, symbols/motifs, contact/gaze, interpersonal distance, and shape. As an example, she quoted Serafini's (2014) point that symbols and motifs are "constructed in the social contexts of their use and conventionalized over time" (p. 61–62) and then explained that the broken clocks in the story are a symbol/motif. This student wrote, "Besides representing Hugo's passion for horology, a broken clock can also mean that a person has unresolved issues of the past [or a] disregard of the passage of time...Hugo desires to return to his joyful past with his father still alive." Li realized that in this book, "both mediums of communication, written literature and illustrations, create a synergistic and complementary effect..., which forges a lasting impact on the reader."

Using Visual Storytelling to Support Democratic Approaches to Literacy Instruction ▪ **63**

Figure 4.2 Going to the U.S. comic.

For the comic/zine assignment, Li composed a comic about immigrating to the United States from Singapore (see Figure 4.2). This story shares her experience coming to this country. In the comic, Li uses a variety of visual elements, including color, shape, symbol, contact/gaze, and size/scale. Below are three examples:

- **Color:** I used a blue background in several panels to show that I am comfortable and stable in my environment. There is only one panel that has a grey background, and it conveys my... sadness. Orange, which is often used to convey the changing of seasons, illustrates that my life is about to change drastically from that point onwards.
- **Shape:** The faces of the characters are circular in order to communicate a sense of friendliness and comfort to the reader.
- **Symbol:** The sunflowers I used symbolize good luck and lasting happiness in Chinese culture. The placement of the sunflower indicates that a positive experience awaits me in the future. I also incorporated a butterfly at the end to symbolize my hope, endurance, and courage.

Li put a lot of thought into how to tell her story through visuals. To construct this comic, she first had to figure out how to fit the events into just six panels. This involved deciding which details were extraneous and should be cut. She sketched everything in pencil and then wrote captions for each panel. Finally, she used markers to make the story more vivid.

Reflecting on the value of teaching visual storytelling, Li wrote, "In the current digital world, almost everything is visual... Zines and comics [can be used] to teach students visual literacy [and help students] read... at a more complex level." She added that she planned to use visual tools with students and ask them "about their various interpretations of a story and what they feel about it." She explained, "I want them to know that not everything in the world is as clear-cut as a textbook. Everyone has different opinions regarding a situation and that is completely reasonable." Li believes that students enjoy reading visual texts, and now she has strategies for reaching many kinds of learners. She can also teach empathy through visual storytelling. For this student, visual storytelling offers a path to make literacy learning more democratic by honoring differences and teaching respect for others.

Angelina

Angelina (she/they, her/them) is a 20-year-old student from Bosnia who enjoys reading, writing, bullet journaling, and scrapbooking. In their visual analysis paper, Angelina wrote about *Anya's Ghost* (2011), noting the use of size/scale, symbols/motifs, salience, borders, point-of-view, color, narrative structure, montage, and framing in the book. For example, this student quoted Serafini (2014) to explain that "framing is created by the use of negative space or borders around an object or participant to draw readers' attention to what is in the frame, or how the frame separates certain entities" (p. 65) and then noticed this at work in *Anya's Ghost* (2011) with the "newspaper clippings in the background. Brosgol is emphasizing the article

Using Visual Storytelling to Support Democratic Approaches to Literacy Instruction • **65**

being read as it's playing out, putting literal words into images rather than just Anya reading aloud. It differs between the reality Emily presented the readers and the true and dark story hidden all along."

For the comic/zine project, this student composed a zine about growing up as a Bosnian girl (see Figure 4.3). They explained:

> Bosnia is a rather small country in Europe by the Adriatic Sea, and while it is a very beautiful country, it was not long ago that it was still considered a

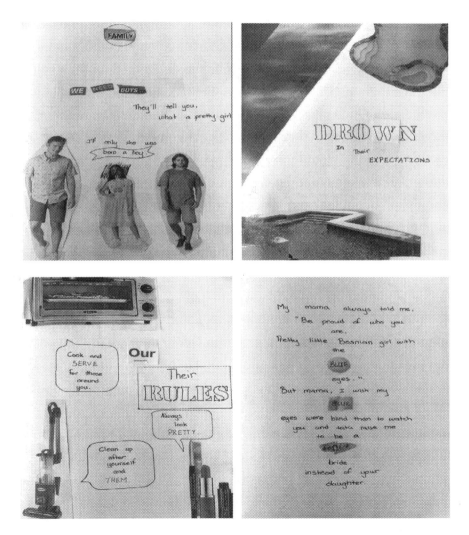

Figure 4.3 Excerpts from Little Bosnian Girl zine.

third world country. [Bosnians traditionally have the] point of view [that] women [are] subservient. Boys are preferred and are always in charge. [This zine] covers the misogyny I grew up with and how I struggled with my identity from being proud of who I was and my ethnicity but also [feeling] ashamed because... I morally disagree with [these traditions and cultural norms].

This student used construction paper, tape, stencils, and photos from food magazines to make this zine. According to the artist statement, they considered a variety of art and design elements while putting together the project, including size/scale, color, framing, contact/gaze, and information zones. Below are three examples:

- **Color**: Pink [is used for] the capitalized words, "SERVE," "PRETTY," and "THEM," which is supposed to reference toxic femininity and classic gender roles that young girls are forced into.
- **Framing**: [Framing is used] on the pages for "DROWN in their expectations" where images of water and pools surround the phrase, quite literally drowning the words while being spoken, or the way the words "OFF" are placed all around the posing women's bodies on another page, depicting the vulgar demands of toxic masculinity to make the reader feel cornered or trapped.
- **Contact/Gaze**: The women's faces aren't included in the pictures, portraying their only worth being in their bodies and nothing else according to the male gaze. This also applies to the crossing out of the young girl's face on the page saying, "If only she was born a boy."

Angelina's "Little Bosnian Girl" zine shows how visual forms can be used not only for personal reflection but also to critique cultural norms that perpetuate inequality.

This student sees the potential for using zines in education. Making "creative projects like this helps encourage students, especially artistic ones, who are unable to express themselves properly through standardized tests." Angelina recommends that visual works be used in all subjects, not just English classes, because they encourage "individuality," making space for students to "think for themselves and learn more about their interests." Opening up English education spaces to honor students' interests makes literacy learning more democratic.

DISCUSSION

In regard to the first research question, this study found that participants learned about a wide variety of visual elements (i.e., dot, line, shape, orientation, narrative structure, information zones, color, borders, contact-gaze, size/scale, salience, symbols/motifs, interpersonal distance, point-of-view, montage, and framing) from reading about these ideas in Serafini's (2014) chapter. The participants were also able to apply these concepts to a YA text they read for the course. Gaining access to a visual vocabulary and learning how particular visual elements create meaning empowers students to read visual narratives more closely.

In answer to the second research question, the participants used a variety of visual elements (i.e., color, dot, line, size/scale, typography, shape, symbol, contact/gaze, framing, information zones) in their comic/zine projects. These students grappled with how to tell their stories through visual and linguistic modes and made choices about project layout and design (New London Group, 1996). It appears that these participants were able to transfer what they had learned from reading about visual concepts to conducting a visual analysis of a published work to composing an original comic/zine of their own and reflecting on it. This finding is consistent with my previous research (Williams, 2019), and together these studies suggest that using a three-step process to teach visual literacy can be effective in both face-to-face and online settings.

IMPLICATIONS

Based on this research, a three-step process for teaching visual literacy is recommended. First, students compile a toolkit (New London Group, 1996) of visual concepts. Serafini's (2014) book is a wonderful resource for making sense of visual narratives in print form (e.g., picturebooks, comics, graphic novels), animation, and videogames. Other handy resources are available by Eisner (2008), Bang (2016), and McCloud (1993, 2006). For making sense of live action works, I recommend the Columbia Film Language Glossary (https://filmglossary.ccnmtl.columbia.edu/term/) and Appendix A of Golden's (2001) book.

After students learn about visual elements, the next step is to ask them to examine visual narratives. In a face-to-face course that meets for a full semester, my students and I look at several examples of visual narratives and discuss them together before I ask them to write a formal visual analysis paper. Identification (matching visual terms to examples in the narrative) is a basic part of this work but not an end-goal. Students need to go beyond that and explain *how* particular visual choices communicate meaning at a particular moment in a story. In their papers, students include photographs or screenshots from the visual narrative, so the exact moments they are writing about are clear. I also expect them to write about at least three visual elements per image (three images = nine elements), quote from the visual resources I have provided as they define their terms, discuss specific details in the image, and comment on the ways that these design choices contribute to or advance the story.

The final step is to give students a chance to compose an original visual narrative that makes use of the visual elements they have learned about in the course. I also ask them to reflect on this work in an artist statement. In the statement, they summarize the story (the plot is not always obvious), identify five visual elements used and how those choices communicate information, and reflect on their process and tools. Sometimes I will ask students to include two photographs showing their project at different stages; I think this is fascinating to see, and it provides some evidence that the work is theirs. However, this particular comic/zine project had to be hand-drawn, so I did not include this requirement this time. When teaching pre-service teachers, I do recommend having a fourth section of the artist statement where they can think about how they could use or adapt this assignment in their own teaching.

CONCLUSION

This study demonstrates that these pre-service teachers benefited from their experiences with visual narratives. They read visual works closely and analyzed them using concepts they had learned in the course. They also composed original pieces, keeping these visual concepts in mind as they told their stories. Every assignment that English educators use with pre-service teachers is a model they can think back to as they plan curriculum for students. It is important to me that pre-service teachers learn some strategies for teaching visual literacy. Their reaction to this work gives me great hope for the future. After all, they noticed the potential of visual storytelling for building students' visual literacy skills, making reading more accessible to students, and teaching empathy.

Visual storytelling can help make English classrooms more democratic, especially when working in tandem with inclusive literature and opportunities for student decision making and creative expression. Comics and zines are engaging forms that encourage reflection, critique, connection, and imagination. These kinds of arts-based writing assignments also open up spaces to honor students' cultures, languages, interests, and experiences. One of my favorite things about teaching visual storytelling is the way that it can shift the balance of power in a class. Students take charge and make decisions as writers and artists. As an English professor (not an art professor), I am in many ways a fellow learner. I find this shift incredibly refreshing and exciting, and my students' creativity never ceases to amaze me.

ACKNOWLEDGEMENT

Thank you to Mandy Hall, MA student in Narrative Studies at Arizona State University, who served as a teaching assistant in the ENG 471 course described in this chapter.

REFERENCES

Bang, M. (2016). *Picture this: How pictures work*. Chronicle Books.
Council of Writing Program Administrators, National Council of Teachers of English, and National Writing Project. (2011). *Framework for success in postsecondary writing*. http://wpacouncil.org/framework.
Eisner, W. (2008). *Graphic storytelling and visual narrative: Principles and practices from the legendary cartoonist*. W.W. Norton and Company.
Golden, J. (2001). *Reading in the dark: Using film as a tool in the English classroom*. National Council of Teachers of English.
Guzzetti, B.J., & Gamboa, M. (2004). Zines for social justice: Adolescent girls writing on their own. *Reading Research Quarterly, 39*(4), 408–436.
Klein, S. (2010). Creating zines in preservice art teacher education. *Art Education, 63*(1), 40–46.
Kwon, H. (2020). Graphic novels: Exploring visual culture and multimodal literacy in preservice art teacher education. *Art Education, 73*(2), 33–42.
Lee, S., & Buscema, J. (1978). *How to draw comics the Marvel way*. Atria.
Maliszewski, D. (2013). The benefits of writing comics. In C.K. Syma & R.G. Weiner (Eds.), *Graphic novels and comics in the classroom: Essays on the educational power of sequential art* (pp. 233–244). McFarland & Company.
Marrall, R. M. (2013). Multicultural education through graphic novels. In C. K. Syma & R. G. Weiner (Eds.), *Graphic novels and comics in the classroom: Essays on the educational power of sequential art* (pp. 245–250). McFarland & Company.
McCloud, S. (1993). *Understanding comics: The invisible art*. William Morrow.
McCloud, S. (2006). *Making comics: Storytelling secrets of comics, manga, and graphic novels*. William Morrow.
New London Group. (1996). A pedagogy of multiliteracies: Designing social futures. *Harvard Educational Review, 66*, 60–92.
Park, J. Y. (2016). "Breaking the word" and "sticking with the picture": Critical literacy education of US immigrant youth with graphic novels. *English Teaching: Practice and Critique, 15*(1), 91–104.
Serafini, F. (2014). *Reading the visual: An introduction to teaching multimodal literacy*. Teachers College Press.
Weiner, R. G., & Syma, C. K. (2013). Introduction. In C. K. Syma & R. G. Weiner (Eds.), *Graphic novels and comics in the classroom: Essays on the educational power of sequential art* (pp. 1–10). McFarland & Company.
Williams, W.R. (2019). Attending to the *visual* aspects of visual storytelling: Using art and design concepts to interpret and compose narratives with images. *Journal of Visual Literacy, 38*(1–2), 66–82.

YOUNG ADULT LITERATURE

Brosgol, V. (2011). *Anya's ghost.* Square Fish.
Dembicki, M. (Ed.). (2010). *Trickster: Native American tales: A graphic collection.* Fulcrum Books.
Pérez, C. C. (2017). *The first rule of punk.* Puffin Books.
Quintero, I. (2014). *Gabi, a girl in pieces.* Cinco Puntos Press.
Selznick, B. (2017). *The invention of Hugo Cabret.* Scholastic Press.
Takei, G., Eisinger, J., & Scott, S. (2019). *They called us enemy.* Top Shelf.
Yang, G. L. (2006). *American born Chinese.* Square Fish.

CHAPTER 5

IDEAS UNSCRAPPED

Repurposing Metal to Support Identity Building in Writing

S. Rebecca Leigh

In the language arts methods courses that I teach, I regularly ask my preservice teachers to think about what it means to write to help them name their beliefs about writing. Often, these discussions are challenging and semester-long because they reveal a strong verbocentric ideology (Eco, 1976), the belief that language should be privileged over other ways of knowing, fertilized over the years by a steady diet of worksheets and fill-in-the-blank writing exercises. The overall effect of such writing practices can be seen in rather dismal past and current reports from the National Assessment of Educational Progress (National Center for Educational Statistics, 2012) where many children are below grade-level proficiency (Salahu-Din, Persky, & Miller, 2008), where writing has been deemed a neglected skill by the National Commission on Writing (NCOW, 2003) that continues to be a challenging subject area for teachers of writing (Graham & Harris, 2016).

While my preservice teachers know these statistics and want to disrupt the status quo on how writing is traditionally taught in K–12 schools, many

Cultivating Democratic Literacy Through the Arts, pages 71–86
Copyright © 2024 by Information Age Publishing
www.infoagepub.com
All rights of reproduction in any form reserved.

are unsure how. Their uncertainty is not surprising given the historical pervasiveness of verbocentrism, the positioning of language as "the sole channel for learning" (Siegel, 1994, p. 2). When my preservice teachers share their personal writing histories, many can recall the limiting but all too common phrases "Don't worry about the art" and "If there's time afterwards, you can draw a picture for your story."

Ways of knowing (Berghoff, Egawa, Harste, & Hoonan, 2000) allow us to express ourselves and, when we express our knowing in a variety of ways, one way supports the other. When this happens, we extend our knowing by taking on new perspectives. Each way of knowing (e.g., art, music, math, drama, science, language) also helps us to express ourselves in diverse ways. For example, what we cannot say through words we might express more eloquently through color.

My writing history is not much different from my students' K–12 experiences as writers. As a teacher educator, I share my own feelings of inadequacy that I have felt as a former high school teacher trying to disrupt traditional approaches to writing in the classroom. I share that, in those early days of teaching, I was still learning how to broadly define literacy and that I had much to learn about the symbiotic relationship of art and language and how all ways of knowing are cultural and personal channels through which meaning is constructed and shared.

In this chapter, I share three former literacy practices and how these practices have evolved in my teaching of writing. I couch these examples through my work in the writing clinic, a seven-day summer workshop that is held at a university campus that leads children in kindergarten through grade 8 through artful engagements to support vivid and descriptive writing. Through these discussions, I help my preservice teachers interrogate their beliefs about writing by a) showing them examples of what children are capable of writing when the invitation to write involves the aesthetic and b) sharing the mindset shifts that I had to make in order for this to happen. In the paragraphs that follow, I first provide some background about the clinic and the lessons, followed by three sections each beginning with the phrase, "I used to" that speak to former literacy practices of mine.

THE WRITING CLINIC

The writing clinic, offered the last week in July at a university in the Midwest, includes six two-hour instructional sessions and an author's chair celebration on the seventh day. It does not take a diagnostic approach to writing; rather its mission is to help young children discover the joys that come from writing practices that build art into literacy learning (Olshansky, 2008; Ray, 2010).

Some researchers may narrowly define literacy as the ability to read and write but the writing clinic, steeped in a twenty year history of building art into its 7-day workshop, is grounded in the belief that literacy is more than writing and includes other communication systems such as the visual arts. Most children, particularly middle schoolers, find themselves rather surprised and delighted by this. The Artist/Writer Workshop model (Ernst, 1994; Olshansky, 2008), influenced by the writer's workshop model (Atwell, 1987; Calkins, 1986; Graves, 1983), identifies through research-based studies the importance of having artful conversations and experiences in writer's workshop to discover and develop power of expression in writing. The writing clinic follows this model.

For the last three years, children in the clinic have been painting on 16-guage weathered steel, fashioned by a local manufacturer into a 1" × 1" square with a hook welded on the back. The purpose of the research was to investigate how painting on steel, a porous medium that absorbs and therefore changes with each paint application, could spark for children original ideas for writing, yes; but more importantly, that it could help them experience revision as a positive experience by revising their stories based on the systematic changes that each steel draft presented. As paint, water, and sand helped to illuminate the imperfections and serendipitous rust markings of metal so, too, could children feel the invitation to revise their writing in both content and style based on their observations of these changes. In the clinic, working with steel created a pathway for developing comfort with and an interest in revision in writing.

During this same time, and in response to a growing clinic demographic, more culturally relevant texts with craft-like narratives and compelling illustration were infused into the lessons on painting with steel where children were provided opportunities to 'meet' diverse characters through a windows/mirrors framework (Sims Bishop,1990) where readers can see themselves and others reflected in the characters and storylines in the books they read or that their teachers read to them. The children delved into painting, poetry and personal narrative writing –ideal genres for manifesting a sense of identity (Calkins, 1986).

WRITING CLINIC LESSONS OF ART AND LANGUAGE

The structure of the daily lesson included:

- a "wicket" or word, drawn from a word well (Leigh, 2014) to be considered for one's writing. In this chapter, examples of wickets in Figures 5.1–5.4 are in boldface;

- a discussion of an illustration technique from Katie Wood Ray's (2010) "In Pictures and In Words" such as 'crafting an ending that returns to the lead' or 'shifting tone by shifting color';
- an exploration of identifying the technique in several texts by different authors;
- a free-write (Murray, 1987) to practice the technique in the writer's notebook as a process for developing and cultivating ease with author's craft experimentation;
- a read aloud from a culturally relevant text;
- a balanced discussion about the rich language work in the read aloud (i.e., where do they see the technique and other examples of beautiful language) and about the illustration, often applying Molly Bang's (2000) principles of how pictures work that gives children the language of the artist (e.g., where do they see contrast and how does it enable them to see, where do virtual shapes imply energy, etc.) to talk about how pictures enhance meaning in texts;
- a "free-paint" on a steel canvas, much like a free-write or free-draw, where children could apply some of Bang's principles to their design decisions and color choices as inspired, perhaps, by the discussion on the illustration art from the read aloud;
- a block of time for independent writing to develop writing as influenced by the physical imperfections and markings from the steel canvases;
- a small group sharing where they could see and hear aspects of each other's work;
- a walk-through of a cordel, a string stretched across the classroom for hanging text (e.g., lifting a line from a book to better appreciate the language) and art (e.g., close up picture of a character's face to better appreciate techniques used) that supports engagement with challenging texts, whether individually, in pairs, or small groups; and
- an informal interview one-on-one with me, a 5-minute conversation to understand their 'creative moves' in their work including what theory of writing they hold for themselves.

Each following day, the children participated in a gallery walk of rows and rows of steel canvases. This walk invited discussion about how the wet and colorful steel from the day before, now dried and partially rusted, manifested new directions and possibilities for revision that supported the physical changes of the metal. Each canvas, and poem or personal narrative, underwent three to four revisions of painting and writing per child. In these lessons, the children experienced the meaningfulness in creating and close-attending to visual texts and how this closeness supports not only strong writing (Albers, 2007) but also helps illuminate how a culturally relevant text can cultivate discovery of self and other through one's writing.

In the paragraphs that follow, I identify three former literacy practices that I have shared with my preservice teachers, each beginning with the phrase, "I used to," and how these practices have evolved in my teaching of writing, couched in examples from the writing clinic, and each beginning with a quote from a child in the writing clinic to help contextualize each section.

I Used to Hurry the Art During Writing Time

> *I loved painting on the steel because it changed every day. It's unique every time. And I took risks with the steel that I wasn't thinking of taking that helped me with my writing.*
>
> —Hanna, grade 8, interview response

Looking back on my teaching of writing, whether at the secondary or university levels, art-making has consistently been at its core. I encouraged practices that invited students to take risks in their work, through art-making and writing; however, I placed a premium on risk-taking in writing. For example, I cheered when a student changed the genre of their piece that might not have been working in narrative form to, say, poetry or song lyrics. I smiled when a disengaged writer, in particular, suddenly incorporated an example of author's craft into their writing that they had resisted many times before. I hurried our art engagements to get to the writing where they could experience for themselves the "risks" that I appreciated in writing. This hurrying was, perhaps, my biggest mistake. And it communicated to the classroom the opposite of what I valued and stood in stark contrast to the generative theory of literacy that I thought I held for myself.

I underestimated how risk-taking in art, for example, could *drive* strong writing rather than simply *inspire* someone to write. And by strong I mean what Fletcher (1999) means: "the kind of writing that has a current running through it—energy, electricity, juice" (p. 3). I drew upon arts-based literacy theory as a way to understand these differences. Hanna's (all pseudonyms) conversation with me in the writing clinic eloquently illuminates the difference (see Figure 5.1). In this interview, Hanna had just completed Grade 9 and had therefore aged out of the clinic; however, having regularly participated in the clinic many years before, she desired to return and was welcomed as a returning writer who enjoys the aesthetic.

Hanna was more than simply inspired to write. She noted the difference between writing from 'doing something creative' and delving—if not 'diving'—into a complex creative process that 'challenges,' and invites 'honest' and 'raw' work. She actively engaged in art and through art discovered

76 • S. R. LEIGH

> **Me:** When do you feel good about your writing?
>
> **Hanna:** When it truly reflects how I feel on the inside. When it's honest.
>
> **Me:** What helps you get to that place of honesty in your writing?
>
> **Hanna:** Sometimes I doubt what I say in my writing but the art that we do helps a lot. In school, it's very forced like 'write a topic about nature' rather than going out and actually seeing nature. I get excited about poetry units in school and then I'm like, this isn't poetry. I mean, it's poetry but it isn't. But painting on the steel is exciting because it's always changing so it feels like a place where you can find honesty and write from that.
>
> **Me:** That's interesting to me. Can you talk about this some more?
>
> **Hanna:** It's like waiting for you, you know?
>
> **Me:** What's waiting?
>
> **Hanna:** All of these challenges. The opportunity to be honest, to be raw. You can be afraid of it or you can just dive in and experiment. I think you can get real when you dive. In school, I don't reveal myself on the page because I feel like it's not an environment where I can reveal myself.
>
> **Me:** So would you say you don't 'dive' in your writing at school?
>
> **Hanna:** Exactly. I mean, we might get an idea [for writing] from doing something creative and that's fine but that's not necessarily where you can be honest in your writing, where it lives, not for me anyway.
>
> **Me:** Where does it live for you?
>
> **Hanna:** [laughing] in the steel paintings! I've taken risks with the steel that I never thought I'd do and I've wrestled with it and loved it and tried new things with it until I [could] see and feel something. And I think that shows in my writing this summer.

Figure 5.1 Hanna's perspective on taking risks in art.

her growth as a writer but also what Eisner (2002) has long maintained: to express oneself in art is different from other modes of representation such as language. Her peers shared similar perspectives: "When you don't know what you're doing in art you have to use your own imagination. Nothing is a mistake—like when I use extraordinary words and adjectives I know it's because of something that I did in art that helped me" (Jim, grade 4).

I tell my preservice teachers that in arts-based literacy, children need time to develop their art. This is what happened in the writing clinic: some children spent a little more time on their steel drafts but being invested in their painting—making deliberate and thoughtful content decisions about a particular paint color, for example—often lead to some terrific gains in their writing such as how a color could provide the backdrop to a particular style and tone in one's narrative. Such visual/verbal connections are clear, for example, between Dan's steel painting in burnt umber and sienna (see Painting 5.1), earthy color choices inspired—as shared with me in our interview, by James Ransome's color palette in Woodson's (2002) *Visiting Day*

Ideas Unscrapped • 77

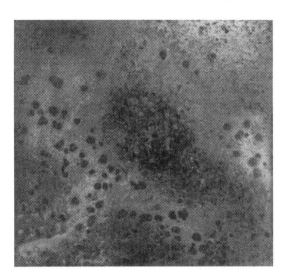

Painting 5.1 Dan, Grade 4, Experimenting with brown paints.

and Mary O'Neill's (1967) meditation on 'what is brown' in *Hailstones and Halibut Bones*, and his poem in Figure 5.2.

Just as in writer's workshop not all children are drafting on the same day, the same principle is applied to the writing clinic; some children worked on their steel drafts whilst others worked on their poems or narrative drafts, taking chances in both. To look at their final written pieces, one could not tell who worked on their steel drafts longer than others, an observation that begs the question for my pre service teachers: "If we cannot tell, why, then, do we as teachers worry so much about children spending too much time on their art? If their art-making can yield a visual so rich and engaging that it helps give the artist ideas for beautiful written language, why worry?" To illustrate this point, we talk about the common fears associated with doing an aesthetic engagement in a writer's workshop. "There won't be enough

> "She's warm and brown. Awesome. **Pure.**"
> A feeling, a friend,
> a stone calling home.
> Brown is baked apple,
> and a caramel for two.
> This I know for sure.

Figure 5.2 Dan's Brown poem.

time to write," many say. Indeed, we often hurry an artful practice, as I used to do, because we think that having more time to write will lead to better writing. "We don't know how to talk about art in meaningful ways," say others in my class. This is an important conversation with my preservice teachers because it helps them to understand that they can talk in comfortable and confident ways with children about what makes pictures captivating (Bang, 2000), and that they can effectively audit their workshop time so that it protects space for writing. Some children will stay longer in their art-making than others but, and this is key, if children are shown systematic ways to make their art more visually compelling, such an investment can and will show up in their writing (Albers, 2007; Olshansky, 2008; Ray, 2010).

I Used to Privilege the Writing Over the Art in My Read Alouds

> Talking about art elements in picture books has really helped me to understand how illustrators build emotion and mood and things like that. It's empowering to feel like I can show kids an exciting way to make their writing more descriptive—not through another lesson or strategy, but a conversation.
>
> —Kelly, preservice teacher, exit slip response

Indeed, a conversation with children on what we notice, together, about how illustrators use visual devices to draw them into pictures – devices such as using a thick line to express a sense of power or a circular line to express energy, unity, or warmth (Bang, 2000) – and how the level of detail in a picture can affect our attachment or interest to any given page (Ray, 2010) can be empowering; it gives children the language of the artist. More than this, however, it invites children to think about how art can impact language in terms of tone and word choice. For example, when looking at a foreboding scene in a picture book and being able to identify how an illustrator has used dot, line, shape, etc. to render such a scene, what kind of word choices do these art elements conjure up for us as writers? Which strong verbs come to mind? What kinds of vivid and descriptive words can we think of to describe what we are seeing? What literacy devices might we think of, inspired by the illustrator's moves, to draw readers into our own stories?

I did not always know to ask these kinds of questions. In those early years of my career, I was narrowly focused on the literary devices that authors use (e.g., a carefully chosen quote, dialogue, description, and compelling narrative voice) to lure their readers that I overlooked picture book illustration that helps carry some of the emotion and context for a story. Often, I would remark on a 'beautiful page' but I did not draw their attention to what made a two-page spread particularly beautiful or eye-catching. I glossed over art

Ideas Unscrapped • 79

elements and principles of visual design in picture book illustration, not realizing the connectedness between artful talks and strong writing. In privileging the discussion about the rich language work that I saw in a picture book, and not participating in any close-attending to the visual text as a sign system that communicates its own particular ideas (Eisner, 2002), I was contributing to verbocentrism. Even though I was not explicitly saying, "Don't worry about the art," I was still saying it through my demonstrations.

Preservice teachers need opportunities to learn how to read art (e.g., dot, line, shape, perspective, and so on) in picture book illustration, for example, and know how to comfortably apply these artful readings in their workshop lessons with children in ways that actually motivate children to pick up their gel pens and want to write. Molly Bang's (2000) work provides teachers an accessible entrée to talk with children about how an artist uses line, shape, and color to grab and hold one's attention. And children, as well, need opportunities to meaningfully practice vivid and descriptive writing as influenced by the visual texts that they read or that their teachers read to them (see Figure 5.3).

This kind of artful reading of texts can also help teachers to better understand their children's narratives and ways of making meaning, including how the pictorial weight of a picture can speak to a child as a writer.

Writing inspired by Gordon James' illustrations in *Crown: Ode to the Fresh Cut* by Derrick Barnes
"The pink ocean, gentle and **wavy**, felt cold because of the rain pouring white."
　　—Mary, grade 6

Writing inspired by Ron Brook's illustrations in *Fox* by Margaret Wild
"There's a **glove** of music in the crystal cave."
　　—Ken, grade 4

Writing inspired by Shaun Tan's illustrations in *The Rabbits* by Jon Marsden
"Imagine a beautiful heart-smile, a deep-sized earth that's orange lemonade where everyone dances in the sky where music **bakes** and drips."
　　—Franny, grade 4

Writing inspired by James Ransome's illustrations in *Visiting Day* by Jacqueline Woodson
"She's warm and brown. Awesome. **Pure**."
　　—Dan, grade 4

Writing inspired by Shaun Tan's illustrations in *The Red Tree* by Tan himself
"Life changing, legs shaking, as my friend fell down the waterfall. Eyes **zoning**, legs quivering; I jumped down, too."
　　—Jim, grade 6

Figure 5.3 Examples of children's descriptive writing lifted from writer's notebooks.

80 ▪ S. R. LEIGH

For example, after reading Hanna's first draft (see Figure 5.4), which accompanied her steel draft painting in shades of midnight blue (see Painting 5.2), we talked about what impact, if any, Anne Spudvilas' illustrations in Woolvs in the Sitee had on her writing. In Margaret Wild's story, Ben is an orphaned adolescent who confronts his fears where the 'wolves' serve as a metaphor for many things. "I just love the converging lines," Hanna remarked. "With every page turn, she takes you through Ben's emotions,"

> **Moonfed** water
> absorbs into the sky
> reflecting beauty
> If I close my mind
> I disappear
> as the water and sky
> become one night
> I find myself
> wrapped in indigo whispers
> Everything melts away
> as I become part of the **moonfed** brilliance

Figure 5.4 Hanna's poem draft one.

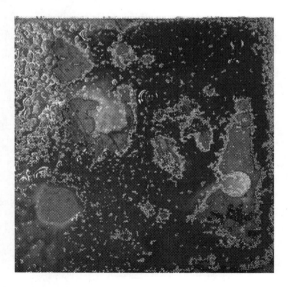

Painting 5.2 Hanna's Midnight Blue painting.

adding, "I felt compassion for Ben. When I drew 'moonfed' from the word well, I thought that was a good metaphor for what I was feeling from these pictures; you can be unsure of where you are and still feel wrapped in something good. I think this first draft captures my mood from those lines." Indeed, Hanna's word choice such as 'indigo whispers' and 'water and sky become one night' is part of the 'juice' in her writing, as Fletcher (1999) would say. In this first draft, the writing is energizing because it is descriptive, delivered in sparse text where every word counts.

In talking about her third draft (see Figure 5.5), we pick up the conversation about the impact of sparseness in art and language, this time with attention to Erika's Story by Ruth Vander Zee which is a Holocaust survivor story. "There's very little writing in Erika's Story, and a lot of repetition, so I experimented with that," explained Hanna. "My steel painting had this new pattern of rust specks in it, too. Kinda like a universe, a repetition of stars maybe." Indeed, what makes her final draft particularly strong is how she uses repetition (e.g., 'no longer' and 'no more') to establish tone and style and idea development—that is, the idea of disappearance (in the first draft) to the idea of acceptance (in the third and final draft). "I think acceptance is powerful, the way Ben accepts his situation and Erika, too. And you can feel that power build in the art, like when it goes from black-and-white to color. Life is like that." Roberto Innocenti's use of grayscale provides a captivating backdrop to the intermittent splashes of pink and full color. "I thought some of the design choices in the art were eerie, like the

> Sometimes I feel like I'm sinking into moonfed waters
> Cracked whispers echo in my mind
> The farther I sink, the more **weightless** I become
> until I start to softly melt into the waters
> melting away from the confinement of reality
> I am no longer in the sky
> No longer in the sea
> Just me
> left to be
> No more sinking
> No more whispers
> No more reeling
> Just an eerie silence
> in a restless universe
> that is now part of me

Figure 5.5 Hanna's poem draft three.

perspective of the train moving away." Together, Hanna and I talked about these observations and where they might have shown up in several drafts of her own work. "I've lost relatives to cancer so I wanted to work with this idea of acceptance. The way the rust came through the blue paint, it looked almost black. And that made me think of the darkness surrounding the train and the darkness that follows it. But there's also this light that feeds you the way a moon can show you the way."

In the writing clinic, using a cordel – that is, a string stretched between two posts for hanging written text and art that I believed would elicit a visual, embodied, or emotional response in the classroom – is where conversations on emotions felt from reading and analyzing certain books could grow. "The cordel is most effective when meaningful work is shared among the students and with a wider audience" (Chisholm & Whitmore, 2018, p. 125). To help my preservice teachers conceptualize this, we set up the same cordel to demonstrate how *seeing the text* (i.e., visual literacies), *being the text* (i.e., embodied literacies) and *feeling the text* (i.e., emotional literacies) supports engagement with challenging texts (Chisholm & Whitmore, 2018), particularly through visual arts-related instructional strategies. This practice was especially important in our discussions of how a cordel can guide children through their close-attending of visual details by walking through, weaving in and out from the hanging pages, to feel examples of self and other by identifying how this is represented in some of the culturally relevant texts that we were reading and studying.

I Used to Assume That My Preservice Teachers Knew the Parallels Between Art and Language

> *I really like the 'access talks' because I can apply what I'm learning in the partnership school and see the results in my child's writing.*
> —Patrick, preservice teacher, exit slip response

Access to complementary forms. Many of my preservice teachers wrestle with the idea that a communication system such as language can be, in any way, complementary to another such as art. This is why, before we even begin a discussion on complementary forms, we first brainstorm together a list of examples of written devices (e.g., compelling narrative voice, description, dialogue, carefully chosen quote, etc.) and visual devices (e.g., color, line, shape, composition, layout, space, texture, etc.) that authors and artists use. Sometimes, we compare styles such as how an artist with a traditional artistic style uses line differently to convey emotion in a picture than a contemporary artist might. When I first started teaching, I did not know to do this.

Over the years, I learned that creating a list like this gives rich and familiar context for a conversation on devices that strike the ear, catch one's eye.

I show them some examples of where parallels can be drawn between devices that writers and artists use to hook their readers/viewers to their verbal and visual texts. For example, I will open to the first page of a chapter book or young adult novel and read one or two opening lines. I do this to engage my preservice teachers in a discussion to help them identify what literary devices an author has used to draw us into the story. Similarly, I will select an illustration from a picture book and project this selected image from a document camera so that we can examine the visual devices more closely and discuss what the artist has done that grabs or hooks our attention. With each demonstration, I invite them to pause and take stock of their own reactions and to talk about how visual and linguistic literacy each have their own potential to communicate particular ideas (Berghoff, Egawa, Harste, & Hoonan, 2000) yet engage in similar and compelling ways. We talk about how this kind of access to meaning making encourages young writers to think about specificity in their work, to decide which device to use over another for a meaningful effect.

Access to parallel structures through cueing systems. Whenever I talk about grammar with my preservice teachers or say words like 'syntax' and 'cueing systems,' I watch them bristle. To avoid this reaction, I now approach the conversation through an artful demonstration by moving around various shapes of cut paper on a document camera to tell a brief story. Molly Bang (2000) is the inspiration behind this practice, using shapes to represent characters from a book. I create and narrate 'scenes' that feel safe and secure (e.g., rounded shapes positioned closely together) as well as foreboding (e.g., pointed shapes with dark backgrounds). As I do this, I explain how perspective and space are examples of using syntax in art. Audible 'oohs' can be heard across the room. This is a much more comfortable entrée into a conversation on how grammar, by comparison, is an example of syntax in language that writers, songwriters, and rappers play with for desired effect. I show them examples of how students in the clinic were able to experience some parallel ways of thinking about art and language through their personal narratives and steel paintings by experimenting with and thinking through both structures – not just writing.

Part of this conversation also helps my preservice teachers see how access to parallel structures is particularly important for struggling writers who experience tensions in one form yet thrive in another (Hubbard, 1989; Ray, 2010). This is where the conversation becomes gritty and for some, uncomfortable. It occurs to some that defining beliefs and aligning practices go hand in hand; it dawns, slowly, that how they define literacy will inform their future lessons and invitations to learn. "If your theory of writing is so narrow such that it only includes pen-to-paper tasks," I say, "what happens to your writers who do not fit inside the proverbial verbocentric box?" Children need opportunities to use what they know in one form (e.g., art, language) to support and grow their knowing in another (Dyson, 1986; Hubbard, 1989; Olshansky, 2008).

Access to process learning. Most of my preservice teachers are familiar with processes in writing and art (e.g., drafting, creating, revising, publishing). Less clear, it seems, is what process learning can sound like. I help bring them into the clinic experience by sharing some of the process decisions that children have shared with me in interviews, depending on their personal goals, visions, and directions for their work. While working on their writing or art, children in the clinic experienced what Murray (1987) means by "a process of discovery" where they used language (and art) as "a tool of exploration to see beyond what they know" (p. 90). What reinforces this idea is their independent decision making; rather than be told what to create or how to revise it, the children had to make these decisions themselves and select the genre (e.g., poem or personal narrative) and techniques with the steel to best showcase their ideas. Their reasons for pursuing one idea over another informed their decision-making rather than determined them. In the absence of prescriptive rules, the students could invest in their ideas, where the judgment arena was less daunting and more intellectual because all decision making was on their terms. This capacity for choice, and having time to practice their choices, is what advocates of the writing process (Atwell, 1987; Calkins, 1986; Graves, 1983; Murray 1987) have long championed, and was fundamental to "being ok" with a degree of uncertainty in one's learning.

CLOSING THOUGHTS

The need for expanded literacy instruction has been widely researched, documented, and supported; however, traditional approaches to writing instruction still exist where many children as writers continue to struggle under the language dominant umbrella – an environment that places a premium on spelling and punctuation knowledge including how and where to apply this knowledge. Is it any wonder that learning to write under such an umbrella might produce so much unimaginative writing? Verbocentrism in schools has limited how children respond to the world, which in turn has limited society's understanding of ways of knowing and why they are used to communicate particular ideas.

The children's commentary on writing represents a call for action to promote the visibility of what verbocentrism in schools looks like and how it affects children's sense of self as writer. The children in the clinic expressed, and rightly so, that writing should be as much fun as it is challenging. Access to arts-based literacy offered them an energizing way of creating and thinking. Children need such opportunities; if they do not, others will make these decisions for them, which is the greatest threat of all to inquiry and the development of one's voice as meaning maker. Continue to challenge norms about writing instruction, I remind my preservice teachers, especially those that privilege verbocentric ideology and perpetuate roadblocks for students who need, and are desperately looking for, engaging entrées into writing.

CHILDREN'S BOOKS

Barnes, D. (2017). *Crown: Ode to the Fresh Cut.* Evanston, IL: Agate Bolden.
Marsden, J. (2003). *The Rabbits.* Vancouver, Canada: Simply Read Books.
Tan, S. (2010). *The red tree.* Melbourne, Australia: Lothian Books.
Vander Zee, R. (2003). *Erika's story.* Mankato, MN: Creative Editions.
Wild, M. (2006). *Fox.* La Jolla, CA: Kane and Miller.
Wild, M. (2007). *Woolvs in the sitee.* Honesdale, PA: Boyds Mills Press.
Woodson, J. (2002). *Visiting Day.* New York, NY: Scholastic.

REFERENCES

Albers, P. (2007). *Finding the artist within: Creating and reading visual texts in the English language arts classroom.* International Reading Association.
Atwell, N. (1987). *In the middle: Writing, reading, and learning with adolescents.* Boynton/Cook.
Bang, M. (2000). *Picture this: How pictures work.* SeaStar Books.
Berghoff, B., Egawa, K., Harste, J., & Hoonan, B. (2000). *Beyond reading and writing: Inquiry, curriculum, and multiple ways of knowing.* National Council of Teachers of English.
Calkins, L. (1986). *The art of teaching writing.* Heinemann.
Chisholm, J., & Whitmore, K. (2018). *Reading challenging texts: Layering literacies through the arts.* Routledge.
Dyson, A.H. (1986). Transitions and tensions: Interrelationships between the drawing, talking, and dictating of young children. *Research in the Teaching of English, 20*(4), 379–409.
Eco, U. (1976). *A theory of semiotics.* Indiana University Press.
Eisner, E. (2002). *The arts and the creation of mind.* Yale University Press.
Ernst, K. (1994). *Picturing learning: Artists and writers in the classroom.* Heinemann.
Fletcher, R. (1999). *Live writing: Breathing life into your words.* Avon Books.
Graham, S., & Harris, K. (2016). A path to better writing: Evidence-based practices in the classroom. *The Reading Teacher, 69*(4), 359–365.
Graves, D. (1983). *Writing: Teachers and children at work.* Heinemann.
Hubbard, R. (1989). *Authors of pictures, draughtsmen of words.* Heinemann.
Leigh, S.R. (2014). *Wounded writers ask: Am I doing it write?* BrillSense Publishers.

Murray, D. (1987). Internal revision: A process of discovery. In C.R. Cooper & L. Odell (Eds.), *Research on composing: Points of departure* (pp. 85–103). National Council of Teachers of English.

National Center for Educational Statistics. (2012). *The nation's report card: Writing 2011* (NCES 2012-470). U.S. Department of Education, Institute of Educational Sciences.

National Commission on Writing. (2003). *The neglected "R": The need for a writing revolution.* College Board.

Olshansky, B. (2008). *The power of pictures: Creating pathways to literacy through art.* Jossey-Bass.

O'Neill, M. (1967). *Hailstones and halibut bones.* Doubleday.

Ray, K.W. (2010). *In pictures and in words: Teaching the qualities of good writing through illustration study.* Heinemann.

Salahu-Din, D., Persky, H., & Miller, J. (2008). *NAEP 2007 writing report card for the nation and the states.* National Center for Education Statistics.

Siegel, M. (1994). *Metaphor and the curricular possibilities of transmediation.* Paper presented at the American Educational Research Association Conference, New Orleans, LA.

Sims Bishop, R. (1990). Mirrors, windows, and sliding glass doors. *Perspectives, 1*(3), ix–xi.

CHAPTER 6

WOOD AND WORDS

Woodworking as an Analogue for Teaching and Writing

Lee Douma

PART I: BURNING WOOD AND TEACHER BURNOUT

There's nothing quite like a toasty wood stove on a cold winter day. We've heated our house with wood for 20 years now—ever since we moved into the farm house that had belonged to my wife's grandparents. I grew up in a home with a woodburning stove, and ever since my early years, I've enjoyed basking in the warmth of a fire in the middle of a cold, dreary winter. It's a reasonable substitute for the mood-elevating sunshine of summer. As a kid, I griped plenty about the hours spent cutting, splitting, and hauling wood to fuel our wood stove, but even then I was fascinated by the beautiful patterns that are revealed when wood is split—the growth rings, the varied tones in different species of wood, the iridescent rays that glisten in a split piece of oak.

Gathering firewood is a simple process, but it requires a high degree of commitment. Those civilized suburbanites who are accustomed to tapping the thermostat for a few extra degrees have never experienced the additional warmth that radiates from inside of a person who has invested countless hours of sweat and strain for their heat. My dad always talked about how firewood heated you three times—when you cut it, when you brought it in the house, and when you burned it. The way we do things, Dad's math undersold the labor. By the time we burn a single small piece of split wood, it has been lifted it at least seven times—from the ground to the trailer, from the trailer to the splitter, from the splitter to the drying stack, from the drying stack to the trailer, from the trailer to the garage, from the garage to the rack in the house, and finally from the rack in the house to the wood stove. I suspect that thorough calculations would push the cumulative lifted weight of a season's fuel to several tons. Burning wood will keep you fit, spare your wallet, and warm your backside on a chilly January night.

Although I had long admired the natural beauty of the wood that I gathered, it wasn't until a few years ago that I thought seriously about making something out of it. By that time I had dabbled in woodworking for several years, but I'd always bought my project lumber from the big box stores. For some reason, milling my own wood had never crossed my mind.

Then one sunny fall-break day in 2017, as I ran a few hundred pounds of dense, high-heat black locust logs through the splitter, I decided that some of it was just too beautiful to burn. Many people don't realize just how much variation there is from one species of wood to another as far as its density, appearance, splinteriness, and splitability. Black locust is my firewood of choice. It is among the densest of North American hardwoods, and density is the main factor in determining the number of BTUs (British Thermal Units) that a species of wood will generate when burned. A piece of black locust will generate almost twice as much heat as a similarly sized piece of cottonwood, for instance. Black locust also burns very cleanly, as opposed to elm and cherry, which tend to leave more soot on a woodstove's glass and in the chimney. A clean burn also means less chance of a chimney fire. Luckily for us, the small patch of woods on our family farmland has more than enough locust to heat our home for many years.

Anyway, on this sunny October day, I decided to make something more than just heat with these beautiful chunks of tree. I split several pieces of black locust into squared off chunks and set them aside while I pondered what to make. I don't remember what other products I considered, but eventually I decided that the best fit for a piece of wood this size was a wooden spoon. The problem? None of the woodworking I'd ever done had involved hollowed-out spaces. Woodworking tools are usually quite specialized, and I had no gouges or other tools for hollowing out bowl-shaped spaces.

Luckily for me, my epiphany about spoonmaking coincided with the rise of Instagram. One of the few benefits of social media is that it allows for sparsely scattered people with similar niche interests to find each other. I dove deep into the world of spoon-carving. There was so much more to that world than I had ever imagined.

As I studied the design of the expert carvers' tools, my cheapskate brain formulated ways to ensure that this hobby didn't take a disproportionate scoop out of my meager teacher income. I was raised in a family that scrimped. There was no chance I was going to spend $40 or more for a hook knife.

I decided to improvise.

I stood in my garage, scanning the walls and shelves with my MacGyver eyes, looking for some combination of scraps and unused tools that could be repurposed. Finally, the image crystallized in my mind. I removed a dull blade from my hacksaw. Due to the aforementioned scrimpiness, it was long overdue for replacement anyway. I proceeded to mount my belt sander upside-down in my bench vise and sand a sharp edge along the blade before cutting off an emery-board-sized piece, which I then bent into a loop. I then crammed the loose ends of the loop into a hole I had drilled in the end of a foot-long dowel rod.

Sure enough, a quick feasibility test on a soft piece of pine confirmed that my design would work. The divots it made were certainly not pretty, but they eventually combined to make a decent, curved hole, which was all that I needed. The inverted belt sander enabled me to shape the outside lines of the spoon. When everything was roughed in, I gave it a final sanding with yet another emblem of my miserliness—a 30-year-old, drill-mounted flap-sander left behind by my wife's grandfather when he passed.

My first several spoons were far from Instagram-worthy, but I kept tweaking my technique. I also kept studying the various nuanced designs of the veteran spoon-carvers on Instagram. I began to notice the subtle distinctions that defined the various factions within the surprisingly robust spoon-carving subculture. There were the purists who carved only with hatchet and knife; there were those who used power-carving burrs, and there were those renegades who dared to cross over boundaries and use a combination of power tools and hand tools.

I most admired the purists, but even in that territory, there were additional practices that further separated the carvers into smaller contingents. There were those who would carve the entire spoon while holding the wood in their hands, and there were those who used bench vises. Then there were those who used a spoon mule. A spoon mule is a specialized seat-workbench combination that consists of a small bench that a carver straddles while facing a raised wooden vise. The two pieces of wood at the pinching end of the vise extend down to the floor so that the carver can activate the tweezers-like pinching action by pushing outward on them with his or her feet. A spoon mule looks awkward and confusing until it's in use by a skilled craftsman. Then it becomes an instrument of great finesse.

I decided I was a mule man.

Once that decision had been made, I had a few options: Option 1: buy one from Michigan Sloyd, the soft-spoken, bearded woodsman from my home state; Option 2: Build my own mule using plans purchased from Michigan Sloyd; Option 3: Cobble together a shoddy mule using various scraps of lumber I had from various projects over the last few years. My scrimpy tendencies won out again, and I began to cobble.

Within one weekend of trial and error, I was able to produce a spoon mule fit for Sancho Panza. But it worked. It held the would-be spoons firmly in place while I carved and gouged away with my homespun carving tools. For the next few weeks, if I wasn't working or grading, I was mounted on my mule, hacking and shaving through another piece of salvaged firewood.

Let's Take a Few Minutes to Discuss Where I Was in My Teaching Career at This Point

Although I'd done some subbing in the spring of '93, after graduating mid-year, I didn't dive deep into teaching until 1994. Bill Clinton was president, and some young upstarts in Silicon Valley had turned *startup* into a household word with the launch of Netscape—what they called a "web browser." The job market for teachers was quite tight at the time. I hadn't been able to land a full-time position, but my wife, an elementary teacher, was offered a first-grade classroom in Goshen, Indiana. We rented an apartment nearby, and I worked as a sub in the Goshen middle and high schools, taking assignments almost every day.

The substitute-teaching experience mirrored the process of carving those first few spoons. It gave me a chance to experiment with various classroom management tools and to figure out what angles of approach led to the smoothest, most effective outcomes. Finally, late in the year, I landed a gig as a maternity-leave sub for a seventh-grade science teacher. In accepting this position, I became part of an interdisciplinary team that met every day. We would discuss what was going well and what was crashing and burning. We'd commiserate about the challenges of dealing with Shawn. We'd plan interdisciplinary units. Some days we'd just drench our exhaustion in laughter while the math teacher told jokes in his brilliantly dead-pan delivery.

My seven weeks in that position went reasonably well, but there were no English positions opening up in that building for the following year. I managed instead to find one a half hour south, in Warsaw. The principal was very supportive and encouraging. Then, three days into the school year, she called me into her office to explain that they'd be adding an eighth-grade social studies class to my schedule. Twenty-some kids were going to be pulled from an overloaded class with a legendary veteran teacher whom they all loved and put in a class with a clueless newbie who had qualified for a social studies teaching minor by taking a few psychology and sociology classes.

Although the principal insisted during my evaluation meeting that I was "a natural," the year did not feel like an overwhelming success. Three or four of my classes were great. The kids were engaged. Rapport was solid. I could let my guard down and enjoy the learning process. Another one or two were okay with the occasional disruption. But that sixth-period class... Oh, my goodness. That sixth period class... It was just about enough to make it a one-and-done teaching career. I don't think there was a single day when I felt like I had a handle on that class.

The next year, a position became available back at Goshen Middle School. I took that position and spent the next five years teaching English, reading, and social studies on two more thoroughly enjoyable interdisciplinary teams. In the last of those years, I taught both social studies and English on a smaller team that received a mandate from the principal to be a project-based class. It was an exciting but busy year. My wife was staying home with our two children under four years old, and I was completing an online master's degree program. Oh, yeah. We were also regularly traveling three hours to the family farm in Waynetown to handle an extensive remodel of my wife's grandparents' 1800s farmhouse.

"The Farm," as it is known to my wife's family, is the only grandparent house my wife has ever known. Her mom's dad had died several decades ago, as had her dad's mom. The remaining spouses then proceeded to get married, instantly turning my wife's already-married parents into step-siblings. This meant that all of my wife's holidays were spent at a single house that contained grandparents from both sides. Grandpa Orval passed away in 1993, and Grandma Mimi moved into a nursing home in 1999. It was at this point that we made the bold choice to move our young family three hours south to occupy the farmhouse that she had vacated. Why we decided that it was wise to commit to a year of three-hour drives in order to remodel a late-1800s farmhouse, I'm not exactly sure. We did, though, which meant that I needed to start searching for jobs.

I spent countless hours carefully aligning response fields of paper applications in the carriage of my parents' Smith Corona electric typewriter. I completed applications for every school district within a 45-minute radius of the farm. It was 2000, and the world-wide web had survived the Y2k threat and grown beyond imagination, as those Netscape guys had said it would. Still, only two of the schools in my search radius had put their applications online by this time. It was clearly a pivot point in the history of school administration. A couple of the fading paper applications I completed for smaller, rural schools appeared to have been created in the 1950s. One of them asked what I was qualified to coach. Among the options: boxing.

I finally took a job at Fountain Central Junior-Senior High School, a rural school with approximately 700 students in grades 7 through 12. I stepped into a position teaching Freshman English and Yearbook. The yearbook advisor I replaced had resigned the position the previous year, when the Josten's rep accidentally erased all of the staff's work while trying to help them back up the files at the end of the first semester.

The professional shift from Goshen Middle School to Fountain Central was significant. Goshen Schools had always been on the cutting edge of educational progress. It seemed that there was a new initiative every year. Although I benefited greatly from some of those programs, the continuous gear-shifting was exhausting. Fountain Central, by contrast, was relaxingly old-school in their pedagogical philosophy. If I wanted to innovate in my classroom, that was accepted, but there was no expectation that I would do anything other than keep the kids under control and make sure that they learned as much as they could. I thrived in this environment where I could sculpt my classroom into whatever shape I wanted. By the time I left FC, I'd also taken on the mass media class, ushering the program into the age of digital video production.

As my oldest child headed into third grade, an English position became available at North Montgomery High School, in our home district. I accepted a position teaching Sophomore English, a couple electives, and Newspaper. This position brought my first opportunity to teach honors classes. I embraced this challenge as a privilege. I sought to engage students in activities involving greater complexity, creativity, and rigor than those of my previous classes. I relished the challenge of getting these highly capable students to make unexpected connections and to explore new avenues of expression.

I moved up to the junior level with that first group of students, which meant a curricular shift to American literature. This job put me in my academic sweet spot, helping students explore the web of connections among philosophical movements, scientific discoveries, political events, and literary texts. Unfortunately, this meaningful holistic approach would come to an end within a few years, when the state of Indiana began issuing letter grades to high schools and basing part of those grades on the number of students who took AP classes. This meant that Junior Honors English would become AP English Literature, and I would now have two trimesters to prepare students for a test that is less concerned with a student's ability to make meaningful cross-disciplinary connections and more concerned with turning students into literary lawyers.

This switch to the AP curriculum was the first of several legislative and administrative measures that would slowly eat away at the creative aspects of teaching that made me love the job. As the emphasis on testing grew in the younger grades, I noticed that students would arrive with less and less interest in creative thought and divergent-thinking activities. In an effort to ensure that we didn't lose touch with the human facets of literary engagement, I began the practice of incorporating structured "enrichment activities" that would engage students in various odd, creative, sometimes embarrassing activities.

Back to the Progress Toward a Spoon Business

At this point, I'd given a few spoons as gifts to family members, school secretaries, and colleagues. The responses had been positive and seemed genuine enough that I decided it was time to begin building a bona fide actual woodworking business. At the point when I made this decision, I had reached the point where I could see myself burning out soon if I stayed in the classroom. I'd been teaching for 25 years—long enough that you'd think I'd be settled into routines that would mean little to no work at home. Although my homework load was certainly lighter than in those first years of teaching, the prep and grading load still filled more of my free time than I wanted to. My hope was that the woodworking income could be one component of a career-transition plan when it came time to leave the classroom.

I knew branding would be a key ingredient in marketing my utensils. Although my spoons were visually superior to an off-the Walmart-shelf spoon, I knew that potential customers would need to see more than just that difference if they were going to pay the prices I'd need them to pay in order to be profitable. I decided that my brand would be centered around the sustainability angle—the fact that I took the wood from tree to final product right here on the farm. I also wanted my packing and labels to look decidedly professional and to capture the aesthetic that aligned with my vision. I talked to a high school friend and graphic designer who graciously worked up the perfect logo for free. I got business cards, started a Shopify website and an Instagram account, and I was on my way.

I was very pleased when my sales reached a couple thousand dollars worth of spoons in that first year. I invested most of that money and a few weeks of labor in the construction of some dedicated, insulated shop space. Having this climate-controlled workspace enabled me to increase my productivity and double my sales the following year. Somewhere along the way, I noticed that the daily school work—the planning and grading—was no longer exhausting me the way that it had been when I first started pursuing this side hustle. The distraction of hands-on work that produced visible evidence of accomplishment had relieved the stress involved with the intellectually oriented work that defined my days.

I believe that my earnings from woodworking this year will equal roughly 25% of my current teacher salary. Although that's not really enough to create the solid career bridge I'd hoped for, I decided a few months ago that this year would be my last in the classroom. I'm not calling it retirement because it's not retirement. I'll still be working more than full time, and I won't receive a pension for several years. Also, I'm not totally ruling out a return to the classroom someday. I'll be finishing out the year and then transitioning to freelance writing work or a full-time job in some sort of business writing or editing. Or it could be teaching online. Or subbing part time and doing some freelance work. Or maybe temping in a factory and subbing and writing. Maybe babysitting? Whatever happens, I know that those chunks of would-be firewood will be covering some of the bills.

PART II—SCULPTING WORDS: HOW WOODWORKING CAN SERVE AS AN ANALOGUE FOR WRITING AND TEACHING

> It all starts in the woods—a whole forest of possibilities. The sun filters through the leaves of the canopy and dances on the forest floor. You're surrounded by weeds, bugs, birds, brush. And wood. Lots and lots of wood. Some of it is in the form of vital, upright trees with all their branches intact. Some of it hangs precariously overhead, debris of a recent storm. Some of it is on the ground, where it has been rotting for years. Some is clearly past the point of being useful for anything other than providing nutrients for tomorrow's trees, but the rest of it is just begging to be shaped into something useful, something beautiful, or something both useful and beautiful. So much raw material. This is where it begins—the material from which so many things in our world are made. And it's all there for the taking.

The topics for writing are limitless—as are the angles from which you can approach those topics. The idea landscape is full of raw material waiting to be manifested as text in some worthwhile form.

Every day, a teacher has countless options of how to approach the content and skills of the day. Although a curriculum map might dictate the core substance of the lesson, an effective teacher will thoughtfully exercise creative freedom with the framing and packaging.

> The more directly you source your material, the greater the overall quality of your final product will be for the end user. If you let others do the initial harvest and milling of your material, the final product will be slightly less "yours."

The written work that is most valued is work from those who have taken the time and the risk to explore new insights rather than repackaging old ideas. The more original a piece of writing is, the more meaningful it will be.

Student engagement with the content will always be proportional to the personal level of investment that the teacher has in the lesson.

> It's crucial for a woodworker to recognize that different woods have different traits. Sometimes what you need is the high rigidity and density of oak or hickory—wood that will hold up to the beating that it will get once it's put out there in the world. Sometimes what's needed is the durability and rot-resistance that comes with black locust or teak. Sometimes you need something pliable and light enough to float on the air if processed properly—like balsa. It's essential that you consider the end user and the end use of your product so that your labor will have been worth the effort.

Effective writers know how to harness and employ the various aspects of language—tone, concision, sophistication, connotations. Writers who attend to these nuances will produce work that withstands the forces in the marketplace of ideas and that has a lasting impact on audiences.

Every class is different and every student is different. Teachers who take these differences into account when planning and delivering a lesson are the ones whose lessons have a lasting impact.

> Some woodworkers are the "fine woodworking" type. These are the ones who measure to the 32nd of an inch and insist upon using the techniques that have been handed down over the years. For these meticulous craftsmen, the dimensions, the angles, the joinery must align with the plans. Other woodworkers are drawn to an approach that is far less structured. They aren't interested in matching the precise measurements and specifications contained on a set of directions. They want to improvise, to follow the grain of the wood toward whatever meaningful forms present themselves. The product of this approach may be a truly one-of-a-kind piece.

Some writers approach the writing process with mathematical precision, crafting for phrases, paragraphs, and logical arguments with air-tight precision. Other writers excel at the use of figurative language, poetic imagery, and emotional appeal to draw the reader into reflection on a topic. There is room in the world for both types of writers.

Some teachers engage with students on a purely intellectual level and are highly structured in their classroom management. Others develop rich personal relationships with students and have a richly emotional connection with their subject matter. There is room in education for both types of teachers. Different instructional and classroom-management styles will resonate with different students.

> In regard to what they do with the pieces they produce, there are people among both of these types who will never sell an item and who will engage in the craft solely because it brings them a visceral sense of satisfaction. Also, there are those who will appear to engage in the creative process for no reason other than to sell sub-par products.

Many of the best student writers—and adult writers—will never publish a word of their writing. They immerse themselves in the writing process simply because the experience of articulating their thoughts brings them a primitive sense of satisfaction.

Teaching: Some teachers are, as confusing as this might be, just in it for the money. They enjoy the predictable paycheck and the security of knowing there will be a pension—albeit a very modest one—at the end of their career. Others teach because they can't imagine themselves doing anything other than sharing their understanding with others.

> Things will always go better for you when you obey the grain. If you try to override the will of the grain and force a line into a weaker part of the wood, your product will strain under the stress of use in the real world. For this reason, it's important to test the product's tolerances during the production process so you can be confident that it will hold up to the stresses of real-world use.

Rarely will a writer reach and impact an audience with a defiant, confrontational tone. It's almost always better to deliver a message with consideration of the audience's existing beliefs and understanding of the world. This does not mean that you don't challenge the reader, but you do so with an understanding of and respect for the relevant schema that exists within the reader's mind. Although it may be easy and satisfying to refute a strawman argument, it's never effective.

Yes, students should respect teachers from the moment they walk in the room. Many of them will. Yes, students should want to learn. Many of them will. Many students, however, arrive in the classroom with no desire to learn anything or respect anyone. A teacher who takes a posture determined by the insistence that students *should* feel or behave in certain ways will fail to reach those students who don't feel or behave in those ways. The chances of meaningful learning and growth occurring is much greater if the teacher is willing to confidently but humbly acknowledge the dispositions that students actually have when they enter the classroom. When a teacher does this, students who were initially defiant or apathetic will often develop respect and a desire to learn.

> Sanding and finishing is key in producing a piece that will not just perform its assigned task but will look good while doing so. It's a hassle to do multiple rounds of sanding between layers of finish, but (at least with certain finishes) it's essential if you want a glossy, uniform finish that accentuates the natural beauty of the grain and will stand up to impacts, water, and other forms of wear and tear.

Writing: When you've finally dumped all of your thoughts onto the paper or screen and done a final proofread for errors, it's tempting to say that it's good enough—to forego those final few rhetorical tweaks. Chances are, however, that the phrases that will have the greatest impact on an audience will be those that get that final bit of refinement—that go from sensible to compelling or from interesting to deeply resonant.

Teaching: When you've been working with a given bit of subject matter for several years—teaching the very same lessons dozens of times—it's easy to forget about the details. It's easy to not update a hook or a pop-culture example.

> In regard to spoon sculpting in particular, the goal is to leave the least amount of material possible while still producing an item that accomplishes the desired task. The handle should be thick enough to be held firmly, the neck should be as narrow as it can be while withstanding the forces it will face in the kitchen, and the walls of the bowl should be as thin as possible in order to allow food to scooped smoothly.

Writing: One of the most important parts of the writing process is the elimination of words that will get in the way of the message. An effective writer knows to leave it lean.

Teaching: The structure of traditional American K–12 schools is outdated and inefficient. An effective teacher bound by the constraints of this system will still do his or her best to keep the actual instruction as lean as possible. This might mean going so far as to write out word-for-word scripts in advance for the most crucial parts of a lesson. The rest of the class time can be spent on practice, immersing students in examples of quality work, and pursuing relevant tangents that build a rich web of context for the skills or knowledge at the heart of a day's lesson.

> Every cook has a unique set of preferences when it comes to wooden utensils. That's okay, though, because there are plenty of distinct utensils and countless variations on each of those. Some people want the tool to be pretty, and some only care about functionality. If you source your material wisely and craft it thoughtfully, it will age gracefully and be useful for many years—maybe even generations.

No writer is universally loved, but almost any genuinely invested writer can find an audience somewhere. When a sentence does find the right audience, it can settle into a reader's mind and provide comfort, clarity, or amusement.

Each student is a unique individual. There is no teacher who will develop a meaningful and lasting connection with every student. Every well-meaning teacher will connect with some students, though. And when that connection is made, the result will last a lifetime.

CHAPTER 7

USING BOOK STUDY TO SUPPORT MULTIGENRE ENSEMBLES IN TEACHER PREPARATION

Pauline Schmidt and Matthew Kruger-Ross

"And now, we have identified that this image is an infographic, right? What is the impact of the image? What stands out? What influences you?" We catch Pauline in guided reflection with our preservice teachers (PSTs) using the Four I Multimodal Strategy (FIMS), a set of interpretive steps that developed from our research into consuming and producing multimodal texts with both preservice and in-service ELA teachers. We co-teach a methods course for second and third year students that focuses on technology and arts-based pedagogies. Our students include future ELA, mathematics, history, and science teachers and therefore our work is uniquely interdisciplinary. Pauline's teacher talk is a reflective snapshot on the infographic in Figure 7.1 that we use to introduce our Book Study assignment, to prepare our PSTs for the books to come. Infographics, as a combination of images and text that communicate a great deal of information, are also excellent

Cultivating Democratic Literacy Through the Arts, pages 99–113
Copyright © 2024 by Information Age Publishing
www.infoagepub.com
All rights of reproduction in any form reserved.

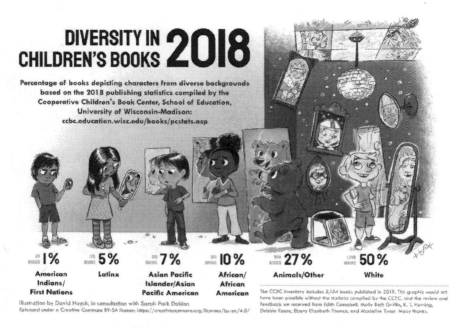

Figure 7.1 Diversity in children's books 2018.

examples of visual texts, of multigenre ensembles that require a redefinition of literacy.

The core of this chapter is informed by a model we developed for consuming and producing multimodal texts via the integration of technologies, or FIMS, seen in Figure 7.2. FIMS represents not only strategies for how to think about texts in ELA classrooms, but also how to teach PSTs to consider how technologies and literacies are intersecting in new and exciting ways. Consider the example that opened this chapter with Pauline's dialogue about interpreting an infographic. The image was chosen purposefully to highlight and bring attention to the inequity in children's book authors with particular attention paid to racial diversity. This infographic is a visual text that not only shares a powerful meaning, but also addresses a key tenet of democratic literacy, as we will see below.

Thus, in this chapter we describe the development and implementation of a course for preservice teachers (PSTs) that aims to cultivate democratic literacy through a multigenre series of assignments called Book Study. The key method or approach to achieve this aim is driven by multimodal, multigenre, and arts-based pedagogies. We include a discussion of our course assignments with specific attention paid to Book Study. In this series of assignments, interdisciplinary groups of PSTs work together to read, review, analyze, and study books that highlight democratic practices and literacies.

For **CONSUMING** texts, teachers lead students through the following practices/stages:
- Identify
- Impact
- Influence
- Imagine

These four practices/stages can be broken down into the following prompts for further reflection and analysis:

Identify. What is it? What do you *literally* experience represented on the page/screen or heard?

Impact. What stands out? What do you first notice? What is striking about the image or sound?

Influence. What is the piece trying to communicate? Who is the intended audience? And why?

Imagine. How can you imagine yourself within the text? Place yourself within the text: Slow down, wonder, pause, let your imagination engage. How can you push yourself to higher order thinking? For example, can you view the text in smaller parts, identify the meaning of these parts and how they might contribute to the overall meaning of the text? *Remember, imagination can seem abstract and broad in terms of application. So, there are no right or wrong answers here.*

For **PRODUCING** texts, we *reverse* the practices/stages:
- Imagine
- Influence
- Impact
- Identify

The reversed strategies can then be broken down into the following prompts:

Imagine. How would you imagine what you are going to create? How would what you have imagined best be communicated?

Influence. What is the best format for communicating your meaning? Who are you trying to communicate to? What do you want to say?

Impact. How can you influence the audience or impact the meaning? How can you best convey the intent of your text?

Identify. Can you identify your successes? Can you reflect on what you did? What did you learn?

Figure 7.2 Four I Multimodal Strategy (Schmidt & Kruger-Ross, 2022).

The books include themes such as voting, democratic processes, critical reflections on American History, immigration and citizenship, and antiracism. We also share specific strategies and activities that emerge from multimodal and arts-based pedagogies that, we argue, are critical in developing democratic literacy in PSTs.

Before moving forward, however, we want to share further on the development of FIMS. Multimodal texts require a transformed understanding of literacies. As teacher educators, we also embrace and advocate for a multimodal lens when approaching literacy; we engage PSTs visually, aurally, and multimodally while acknowledging both analog and digital experiences. We demonstrate this below as we share examples of our work. Literacies, in the plural, signifies that "Literacy is more than reading, writing, speaking, listening, and viewing as traditionally defined. It is more useful to think of literacies, which are social practices that transcend individual modes of communication" (NCTE, 2018). In Figure 7.2, FIMS provides a series of interpretive steps that can be utilized by traditional methods for writing including outlining and reflective pieces, and also includes drawing on key components of the writing process when creating and producing arts-based artifacts such as video and podcast episodes. In our assignments the traditional writing process is mirrored over and over again for our PSTs through multi-genre and multimodal experiences that explore the spectrum between consumers and producers.

Returning to the opening example from the chapter, since Pauline is guiding our PSTs through consuming the infographic (as visual text), she is demonstrating the FIMS consuming strategies. Our PSTs are quickly able to identify the image as an infographic and then she pivots the discussion to the second strategy, impact. One student quickly says "Oh, the numbers..." and Matthew asks for further clarity from the whole class. "Well, 2018 so [the data] is a bit old...but also the percentages...1, 5, 7, 10..." Pauline steps back in from across the room to the third strategy, influence: "Why did the author or designer choose to present this information in this way?" After a few seconds of silence, a male PST responds: "To make us think about why there are so few authors that aren't white." Matthew pushes further: "Future math teachers, based on this data and this representation, how might we make these numbers real and visceral for our colleagues and your future students?" Here we see FIMS in action, from visual text to essential numerical understanding.

These same strategies can be used not only to consume but also to produce multimodal texts, and can also be considered outside the realm of ELA to other disciplines. More will be discussed about FIMS, as well as the Book Study and the connection with democratic literacy, but first we turn to a brief treatment of how we understand and teach with arts-based pedagogies.

ARTS-BASED PEDAGOGY

Elliott Eisner (2002) and Maxine Greene (1995) guide our way of looking at the arts and help us advocate for arts-infused curricula as a means of learning to view the world. Eisner (2002) defines experience as "a process that is shaped by culture, influenced by language, impacted by beliefs, affected by values, and moderated by the distinctive features of that part of ourselves we sometimes describe as our individuality" (p. 1). Eisner makes this social connection when discussing the concept of imagination. He says that it is our imagination that allows us to take risks in the world without the possible ramifications of actually doing that which we imagine. Eisner acknowledges that imagination can be experienced on an individualized basis; however, he notes that it is through a socialization process that we make imaginative contributions to the world. That is, as individuals, we can build on the creation and work of others as we explore our own imagination. Finally, Eisner sees learning as more of a web, with the teacher and students acknowledging that there should be flexibility and improvisation within the realm of learning.

Maxine Greene (1995), in her essays on aesthetic education, likewise states, "We need to have and to teach self-reflectiveness originating in situated life... engaging one another in dialogue" (p. 126) It is this reflective, dialogic piece that is often left out of an educational experience and what is needed for students to have a deeper understanding of their learning, including aesthetic experience through drama and other arts.

This is where and how we see the influence of the arts in a classroom. When we think about our PSTs, we realize "many teachers have little personal experience in the arts and feel anxiety and self-doubt about their personal artistic abilities" (Barnum, p. 125). So, we frame 'consuming' texts with powerful mentor texts to help our students redefine and reconstruct what it means to be an artist. We guide them through a variety of experiences with the goal that they gain "a sense of how successful the use of arts-integrated teaching methods could be in their own future classrooms" (Ames, p. 135). By using FIMS to help our secondary PSTs unpack a variety of texts we are engaging in complex work. "That is the kind of understanding needed for engaging in sophisticated scholarly work, preparing for demanding knowledge-based jobs, and working through the dilemmas of living in democratic societies" (Marshall & Donahue, p. 9). When a teacher utilizes the arts and other modalities of learning, those approaches hold within themselves the true potential for social and intellectual development.

ON DEMOCRATIC LITERACY

While our teaching is informed by arts-based pedagogies, democratic literacies are the highlight of many of the assignments. It is fitting that an edited collection on supporting democratic literacy would be written and published after the historic challenges to U.S. democracy since 2016. Both mainstream news media organizations and academic scholars have discussed, often in minute detail, the status of democratic institutions including elections (Lieberman et al, 2019), public discourse (Gladstone, 2017), and even the nature of fact and truth (Peters, 2017). The general consensus seems at present to be that many of the daily practices and boundaries of society are actually, in fact, simply norms that remain underdetermined within the systems and laws of U.S. democracy. We are faced with three essential questions:

1. What are we to do now?
2. How do teacher educators move forward?
3. And, how do we build greater democratic literacy in our PSTs?

What do we mean by democratic literacy? North (2009) identifies three components: "the seeking of common ground, opportunities for multiple, competing perspectives to be voiced and heard, and discursive, rather than physical, conflict resolution strategies" (p. 563). She also warns that "cultivating sustainable forms of democratic literacy involves considerable alterations of institutional—not merely individual—policies and practices" (North, 2009, p. 573). As teacher educators, then, we must look at our texts and pedagogies to ensure that we are, as North (2009) prescribes, locating the areas where "considerable alterations" of systemic work needs to be done.

But teaching for democracy has a past that begins two decades before the election of the 45th president of the United States. In a thorough and critical summary, Lund & Carr (2008) chronicle the many, many definitions of teaching for and about democracy within educational scholarship that begins in antiracism education (Dei, 1996). They conclude with a checklist that collects the work and recommendations of Banks et al. (2008), organized into Principles and Concepts (see Figure 7.3). These include such questions as "1. Are students taught about the complex relationships between unity and diversity in their local communities, the nation, and the world?" and concepts including Globalization, Sustainable Development, and Identity/Diversity.

Given the complexity of democratic principles and concepts, we have identified three of the components of the Banks et al. (2005) checklist that our course addresses: #6 Prejudice, Discrimination, and Racism; #8 Identity/Diversity; and #9 Multiple Perspectives. The next section outlines how we explicitly address these concepts.

The Book Study

In this third year methods course, we discuss theoretical frameworks for integrating technology into the classroom, and require students to create multimodal projects with a number of digital composition tools. We traverse between and among arts-based pedagogies and digital composition

> **Principles**
> 1. Are students taught about the complex relationships between unity and diversity in their local communities, the nation, and the world?
> 2. Do students learn about the ways in which people in their community, nation, and region are increasingly interdependent with other people around the world and are connected to the economic, political, cultural, environmental, and technological changes taking place across the planet?
> 3. Does the teaching of human rights underpin citizenship education courses and programs?
> 4. Are students taught knowledge about democracy and democratic institutions and provided opportunities to practice democracy?
>
> **Concepts**
> 1. *Democracy*: Do students develop a deep understanding of the meaning of democracy and what it means to be a citizen in a democratic society?
> 2. *Diversity*: Is the diversity of cultures and groups within all multicultural societies explicitly recognized in the formal and informal curriculum?
> 3. *Globalization*: Do students develop an understanding of globalization that encompasses its history, the multiple dimensions and sites of globalization, as well as the complex outcomes of globalization?
> 4. *Sustainable Development*: Is the need for sustainable development an explicit part of the curriculum?
> 5. *Empire, Imperialism, and Power*: Are students grappling with how relationships among nations can be more democratic and equitable by discussing the concepts of imperialism and power?
> 6. *Prejudice, Discrimination, and Racism*: Does the curriculum help students to understand the nature of prejudice, discrimination, and racism, and how they operate at interpersonal, intergroup, and institutional levels?
> 7. *Migration*: Do students understand the history and the forces that cause the movement of people?
> 8. *Identity/Diversity*: Does the curriculum nurture an understanding of the multiplicity, fluidity, and contextuality of identity?
> 9. *Multiple Perspectives*: Are students exposed to a range of perspectives on varying issues?
> 10. *Patriotism and Cosmopolitanism*: Do students develop a rich and complex understanding of patriotism and cosmopolitanism?

Figure 7.3 Checklist for teaching for, and about, democracy (Banks et al, 2005; Lund & Carr, 2008, pp. 11–12)

freely; believing that the analog and digital can benefit and inform one another.

Book Study groups consist of 4–5 PSTs from different subject areas, from ELA, history, and math to science and its subdomains (chemistry, biology, earth/life). These interdisciplinary groups are each assigned a book (see Table 7.1) that they read, review, analyze, and study. Each book highlights a particular angle from which to engage in critical reflection on democratic practices and literacies.

The Book Study texts provide a structure for the PSTs to not only learn the basic techniques and strategies of teaching practice but also introduce

TABLE 7.1 Books and Themes for Book Study Groups

Book	Themes
One Person, No Vote: How Not All Voters Are Treated Equally (2019) by Carol Anderson, with Tonya Bolden	Voting
A Queer History of the United States for Young People (2019) by Michael Bronski, adapted by Richie Chevat	LGBTQIA+
Lies My Teacher Told Me: Everything American History Books Get Wrong/Young Reader's Edition (2019) by James W. Loewen, adapted by Rebecca Stefoff	History, Racism
Stamped: Racism, Antiracism and You/A Remix of the National Book Award-winning *Stamped from the Beginning* (2020) by Jason Reynolds and Ibram X. Kendi	Racism, History
Thank You for Voting/Young Readers' Edition (2020) by Erin Geiger Smith	Voting
Dear America: The Story of an Undocumented Citizen / Young Readers' Edition (2019) by Jose Antonio Vargas	Immigration

them to democratic literacy. To begin, and only scratching the surface, we provide mentor texts for PSTs. We brainstorm, think about, and model how to create text sets with our PSTs. For example, if PSTs are going to teach *Stamped* in their future classrooms, what images (artwork, photography) would they select to use, what podcast episodes (as aural texts such as nonfiction news, narrative OpEd) might exist that can supplement their lessons? PSTs also create digital video reflections on teaching the themes identified from the books in their interdisciplinary teams. All the while, we are constantly referring back to FIMS to help our students understand how these art forms inspired via new technologies are consumed and produced.

As an example of one text set, the *One Person, No Vote* (YA text) Book Study Group paired their study with the MARCH Series (graphic novel) by John Lewis, Andrew Aydin, and Nate Powell. Then, the group located images from the 2020 election in Georgia, John Lewis' home state, of people standing in long lines waiting to vote. And, finally, the group found a podcast episode of Stacey Abrams being interviewed about modern voter suppression. The theme of this text set is access to voting and voter suppression, addressing and highlighting #4 from Banks et al (2005): "Prejudice, Discrimination, and Racism: Does the curriculum help students to understand the nature of prejudice, discrimination, and racism, and how they operate at interpersonal, intergroup, and institutional levels?" Our PSTs used this text set to begin to answer this complex question, a question that is growing ever more important at present. As one student noted at the end of a whole class discussion about utilizing FIMS to analyze Book One of the MARCH Series,

> Sometimes reading graphic novels is looked down upon because they seem like they're 'easy reading' but I noticed when using FIMS that we spent a lot

of time digging deeper and analyzing just looking at two pages. It seems like students would have a much deeper reading experience if they were taught how to slow down and notice, not only the words, but also the way the images and the words interact with each other.

We were proud of the connections this group, and this particular student, made with the texts.

We should note prior to exploring two sample assignments in detail that we rely on FIMS in other ways, too. Not only do we introduce the strategies for consuming to discuss media literacy, for example, but we present PSTs with examples that expressly focus on the process described by the strategies. When we interpret texts and art, we do not move in a linear fashion, step-by-step from identify to impact, influence to imagine. In fact, we jump around and over and over again as we make meaning of what we are seeing and experiencing. This creative process was recently experienced by our PSTs when they found themselves jumping back and forth between the different strategies trying to determine the difference between influence and intention. One astute student asked the room point blank: "When is it influence and when is it impact?" which led to a fascinating discussion about interpreting a visual text!

This playfulness of meaning making occurs in a new way when we approach multimodal assignments and ask our PSTs to consider and enact the producing strategies. We begin now with imagination, and continue forward before closing with identification. FIMS gives us and our students a language to use to describe the creative process, especially when approaching different artforms with new media technologies and platforms. The FIMS language also helps to make concrete this meaning making and interpretive process, an experience that is often quite abstract. When PSTs begin their work in our class and see the kinds of assignments we will be doing they sit in discomfort before realizing that part of our pedagogy is not to merely provide them ideas while we lecture, but rather engage them in embodied experiences as students, before reflecting on the assignments as future teachers. In the next section we describe two of these assignments that focus on aural and multimodal literacy.

Example of Book Study Group Assignment: Experimenting with Aural Literacy–Podcasting

To model and encourage the development of PSTs' aural literacy skills, we have each Book Study Group participate in the creation of a podcast episode that will eventually be published on our podcast series, *Notorious Pedagoges*. Rather than have students draft a traditional book report or research paper after reading their book, we have them create a podcast episode as an aural text. Creating an aural text like a podcast requires students to engage with arts-based strategies for vocalization, like tone and pacing. We hope, of course, that this assignment demonstrates to them that they can have their future secondary students complete a similar assignment, furthering the development of their own aural literacy skills. Consider another Book Study Group that reads *Stamped: Racism, Antiracism and You* by Jason Reynolds and Ibram X. Kendi. The book is a historical retelling of systemic racism in the United States for a YA audience. As to democratic literacy, the text obviously addresses Banks el al's (2005) #6 Prejudice, Discrimination, and Racism. However, the book also takes aim at #8 Identity/Diversity and #9 Multiple Perspectives. These concepts of democracy are elaborated as students grapple with, for example, the distinct identities and rights of a U.S. citizen, refugee, or immigrant, or as PSTs find their traditional understanding of U.S. history challenged by a different perspective.

As PSTs prepare to record and edit their podcast episode, we encourage them to locate mentor texts in other podcast episodes that highlight the authors of their book. We point them to NPR interviews or other popular podcast series that incorporate interviews with some of the authors they are reading. This examination of the mentor text yields multiple benefits; listening to the podcast informs and helps their comprehension of the book, but also can be used as a mentor text for what a good podcast episode sounds like. The PSTs begin to listen like a speaker and creator.

To return to FIMS, as the Book Study Groups begin to edit their podcasts, they must *imagine* how their content can best be communicated. They must continuously understand their *impact* in producing an aural text, a version not meant to be read silently but listened to. By considering the creation of aural texts, we encounter a new and exciting new territory with literacies: reflecting on how to best communicate using our ears rather than just our eyes. To be sure, audiobooks can capture our imaginations and stir our emotions, but how can we prepare students to create and produce podcast episodes that are meant to communicate only via sound? What an exciting challenge!

When we introduce this podcasting assignment, we tell our students more about the history of the assignment and encourage them to listen to past episodes created by former PSTs but of our own solo episodes. Specifically, we ask them to pay attention to tone, pacing, and inflection of the speakers. They have already found a way to represent the content of their books visually, now we ask them to think about the content aurally. We ask them to have a conversation and interview one another about the text. How does this text apply to your classroom? Your teaching?

Here is the list of guiding questions we currently work with:

- When you think about teaching, how does this text inform your practice?
- When you think about the reading we did (Banks et al), where do you see the connection between democratic literacy and your text?
- How might you take what you've learned and translate that to your future classroom for secondary students?

The original intent of the podcasting assignment in our co-taught methods course is not only to expose and teach the technical aspects of creating and producing an aural text, but also to highlight and model how podcasts can be integrated into secondary classrooms. One easy way, of course, is to find ways to have students simply listen to episodes and consume podcasts as aural texts, but we like the added challenge of producing podcasts and not just consuming them.

Example of Book Study Group Assignment: Experimenting with Multimodal Literacy—Digital Videos

Some have argued that the primary challenge to U.S. democracy is a growing distrust of mainstream media amongst a section of the public. Part of the catalyst for this current state of affairs includes the explosion in popularity of social media technologies, as well as increased access to video creation and sharing technologies. Digital video, as a combination of moving pictures that often includes visual and printed text, along with sounds, music, and effects, is a complex, multimodal artform. Integrating videos into the classroom and teaching PSTs to use FIMS consuming strategies is an important step before having students create their own video-based multimodal texts.

In the *A Queer History of the United States for Young People* Book Study Group, the PSTs are charged with producing a digital video biopic of a key figure in LGBTQIA+ history. Before beginning to storyboard their videos, we suggest that they watch a few existing documentaries available on popular streaming sites such as Netflix's *Amend: The fight for America* and specifically Episode 5 "Love." Sharing professional videos is one way to help students see an ultimate mentor text. Within Banks el al's (2005) framework, this assignment and topic focuses on #8 Identity/Diversity: Does the curriculum nurture an understanding of the multiplicity, fluidity, and contextuality of identity? After watching and consuming documentaries made by others, the PSTs are ready to begin the multimodal process of developing their own biopic documentary.

We believe this complex assignment best exemplifies the focus on multimodality not only as a strategy for literacy, but also as a pedagogical tool. For example, we do not have students immediately jump into creating the digital video; we begin first by reminding them of the multimodal literacies required to unpack consuming a digital video and share examples of simple digital video authoring tools. The next step in the digital video project is to have PSTs translate their ideas from notes and additional research into a video script and storyboard. We push students by reiterating the traditional aspects of writing and considering the following questions as they work to produce their multimodal texts:

1. What is the purpose of this piece? *Imagine* who will view/read it?
2. What is your tone? What is the *impact* of altering your word choice when taking the visual and aural pieces and transforming them into a digital video (intended for public consumption)?
3. How can your biopic be framed and produced to *influence* the theme of identity as a democratic concept?

The final step is recording, creating, and editing the video that exemplifies their group's chosen LGBTQIA+ individual. This step likewise falls into a traditional writing workshop format with students collaborating and problem solving together.

The ultimate goal of the digital video assignment is to encourage our students to engage in the production of a multimodal text ensemble that incorporates and intersects with democratic literacy. What is more, we want our PSTs to experience the assignment as a student, but also as a future teacher. We constantly pause throughout the digital video project and ask questions to push their thinking: "How would you adapt this storyboarding for a sophomore humanities course?" or "We've been talking about identity and democratic literacy, but we wouldn't likely use those words with ninth graders. How might you talk about the book in terms accessible for your future students?" The digital video Book Study assignment is but one of the experiences that our PSTs use to explore arts-based responses to topics within democratic literacy.

MULTIMODALITY AND ASSESSMENT

We cannot stress just how important multimodality is in supporting democratic literacies in our work in teacher preparation in mixed, interdisciplinary methods courses. We separate out to visual and aural to explicitly build a strong foundation on which to add multimodality and technology. Our future teachers need to know how to pull apart important texts, like the ones we use in our Book Study Groups.

One of the challenges that comes with being creative and assessing multimodal projects is assessment. Before addressing specific strategies, we must argue for a particular disposition toward assessment. Rather than grading PSTs on products, we try to communicate the importance of the process of their assignments in our course. We are consistently trying to push their thinking as learners and teachers, simultaneously. Since most of our PSTs are coming out of traditional experiences in schools, they are accustomed to mostly traditional assessment methods and we hope to alter their thinking in this way:

> Students demonstrate what they know and can do through an artistic expression—an artwork, a piece of choreography, or a dramatic scene. This alternate way to express understanding is particularly beneficial for students who struggle with traditional paper-and-pencil forms of assessment. Teachers report that they discover abilities and capabilities, which would not have otherwise been revealed, in students who traditionally perform poorly. (Barnum, p. 129)

Arts-based assignments require a transformed understanding of assessment. For us as teacher educators, using technologies and "pure" artforms together are not mutually exclusive.

Ultimately, we adhere to a portfolio-inspired approach where students include various check-ins or benchmarks from assignments to show the progression they've made along the way in completing a particular assignment. Thus, we allow for revisions and resubmissions, treating assessments as formative rather than solely summative. We diligently work to craft clear expectations in assignment sheets and rubrics. We also share examples from previous students to showcase as mentor texts for our PSTs. In some instances we even co-create the rubrics that will be used to evaluate student assignments with and in front of students so that they can have a say in the matter but also so that they can see how we reason as teachers about how to evaluate multimodal projects.

Because this series of assignments occur within Book Study Groups, we have the added challenge of designing effective group work. We build in class time for our students and regularly meet with the students in small groups to check in and assess if they are having any issues. Reflections are key to success; we frequently ask our students to submit short reflections on their specific assignments but also on the process of working together and the group dynamic. We also build in individual and group-based assessments that allow for different levels of assessment, and to honor each of the group members' contributions to the assignment as a whole.

CONCLUSION

We could have included any number of texts as the inspiration for Book Study Groups, but given our shared commitment to social justice education, we knew that we should use our position as teacher educators to highlight and showcase the societal struggles and challenges currently on the horizon in the United States. What is more, we also could have simply required our PSTs to read these books (Table 7.1) in groups and have reflective essays in discussions to further their democratic literacies. But, we raised the bar for ourselves and for our PSTs by having them use the chosen texts to inspire future lesson plans and assignments, and then demonstrated this inspiration through technologically infused art forms including visual texts such as infographics, aural texts like podcasts, and multimodal texts such as digital video.

If we return to the summary of the democratic checklist (Figure 7.3), we can see how, for example, *Thank You for Voting* can be used to inspire digital art forms that can simultaneously address at least #6 Prejudice, Discrimination, and Racism; and #8 Identity/Diversity. In what ways have groups and individuals created and supported institutions, practices, and policies to restrict the right to vote in the past and present within the United States? Think of how an infographic might address and showcase a possible answer. Or, how are the recent 2020 Census data being used to redraw a country with ever-increasing diversity? This might be best addressed in a multimodal text such as a digital video project.

Dear America: The Story of an Undocumented Citizen could inspire critical reflection in all three identified democractic practices: #6 Prejudice, Discrimination, and Racism; #8 Identity/Diversity; and #9 Multiple Perspectives. In what ways has U.S. citizenship been used in the past (and present/future) to discriminate and inscribe systemic racism? How do we, as a country, understand the identity of citizens and the possession of citizenship? How has this changed over time? How can we understand, embrace, challenge, and question the multiple perspectives on questions of citizenship and immigration? All of these questions might inspire a whole class podcast series devoted to offering possible answers to these thick and complicated questions.

Arts-based pedagogies are uniquely poised to help support PSTs development of democratic literacy. Given new opportunities available to teachers and students to create art forms with emerging technologies, the power of the arts to guide our practice grows exponentially. In the end, maybe it is art that can teach us the most about democracy.

REFERENCES

Ames, R. (2016). Prepare the teacher, prepare the student: Arts-based pre-service teacher training. In G. H. Mardirosian & Y. P. Lewis (Eds.) *Arts integration in education: Teachers and teaching artists as agents of change* (pp. 131–144). Intellect. https://doi.org/10.2307/j.ctv36xw21v.14

Banks, J. A., McGee Banks, C. A., Cortés, C. E., Hahn, C. L., Merryfield, M. M., Moodley, K. A., Murphy-Shigematsu, S., Osler, A., Park, C., & Parker, W. C. (2005). *Democracy and diversity: Principles and concepts for educating citizens in a global age.* Center for Multicultural Education.

Barnum, S. (2017). Professional learning in and through the arts. In G. Diaz and M.B. McKenna (Eds.) *Preparing educators for arts integration: Placing creativity at the center of learning* (pp. 125–135). Teachers College Press.

De Groot, I. (2011). Why we are not democratic yet: The complexity of developing a democratic attitude. In W. Veugelers (Ed.), *Education and Humanism: Linking autonomy and humanity* (pp. 79–94). Sense Publishers.

Dei, G. J. S. (1996). *Anti-racism education: Theory and practice.* Fernwood.

Eisner, E. (2002). *The arts and the creation of mind.* Yale University Press.

Gladstone, B. (2017). *The trouble with reality: A rumination on moral panic in our time.* Workman Publishing Company.

Greene, M. (1995). *Releasing the imagination: Essays on education, the arts, and social change.* Jossey-Bass Publishers.

Lieberman, R. C., Mettler, S., Pepinsky, T. B., Roberts, K. M., & Valelly, R. (2019). The Trump presidency and American democracy: A historical and comparative analysis. *Perspectives on Politics, 17*(2), 470–479.

Lund, D. E., & Carr, P. R. (2008). Introduction: Scanning democracy. In P. R. Carr & D. E. Lund (Eds.) *Doing democracy: Striving for political literacy and social justice* (pp. 1–29). Peter Lang.

Marshall, J., & Donahue, D. M. (2014). *Art-centered learning across the curriculum: Integrating contemporary art in the secondary school classroom.* Teachers College Press.

NCTE. (2018). *Beliefs for integrating technology into the English language arts classroom.* https://ncte.org/statement/beliefs-technology-preparation-english-teachers

North, C. E. (2009). The promise and perils of developing democratic literacy for social justice. *Curriculum Inquiry, 39*(4), 555–579.

Peters, M. A. (2017). Education in a post-truth world. *Educational Philosophy & Theory, 49*(6), 563–566.

Schmidt, P., & Kruger-Ross, M. (2022). *Reimagining literacies in the digital age: Multimodal strategies to teach with technology.* National Council of Teachers of English.

CHAPTER 8

FINDING A LIGHT IN THE *NIGHT*

An Opportunity for the Arts to Illuminate the Way

Timothy J. Duggan and Joshua Smith

One issue that is central to our profession as English language arts teachers and teacher educators is the problem of primacy. With insufficient time to prepare new teachers for every possible contingency, we have to ask questions. What is most important for new English teachers to know? What preparatory experiences will be most useful to them as they create their own paths? How do we conceive of and develop practices that allow them to leverage their strengths and, in succession, build the capabilities of their own students? If one of our main goals is to democratize classrooms and develop agency in high school students who often think of education as something that is done to them rather than with them, we must seek to model cooperative, collaborative, and creative ways of being and knowing in teacher education courses. Integrating artistic practices and the dialogue those practices inspire is one way to remove the instructor as the locus of expertise and, instead, to share ownership over what transpires in the classroom—including what counts as knowledge and what work products result from our deliberations—with our students.

Such practices, examples of which we present in this chapter, represent the flipside of the coin of literacy. As English language arts practitioners have recognized now for some time, our notions of what constitutes a text worth classroom consideration have expanded exponentially over the past two decades, and yet the typical high school English reading lists and text types have remained frustratingly stagnant. Likewise, while modes of communication and presentation of knowledge have expanded to include digital texts, multimedia projects, and artistic representations, typical high school English assignments in the age of Common Core continue to be dominated by the argumentative essay. Recent publications have challenged the notion of what students may produce in English class to demonstrate their learning and perspectives on texts they encounter there (Morrell, et al. 2013; Zoss & Macro, 2019). Included in those challenges are calls to expand our range of interpretive "texts" that students produce through their encounters with literature and life.

One question that may be raised in considering an expansion of text types and student work products in English is how practitioners, and particularly ELA teacher educators, may model those practices and encourage our pre-service teachers to experiment with alternative and artistic assignments with students. As such, rather than taking a traditional approach to presenting our discussion for an academic publication, we offer a parallel story of the artistic and pedagogical development of a teacher educator (Tim) and a pre-service teacher (Joshua) that led to Joshua's implementation of artistic practices during student teaching, involving music, visual art, and digital graphic design around a canonical classroom text, Elie Wiesel's *Night*. Understanding who we are and how our identities inform our approaches to teaching and learning will help us to consider how we might liberate our practice from the mundane and create something that resonates with our students and the communities in which we live. We present our individual artistic biographies as prelude to the work that our students have created.

Tim:

I do not come from a particularly musical or artistic family, although my father liked to sing, and he could whistle like a meadowlark. My mother told me that my grandfather had designed cookies for Nabisco back in the 1930s, but he never confirmed the truth of that legend. I learned to play the trumpet in 5th grade and participated in marching band in high school, but what I really wanted was to learn guitar and be like Neil Young.

I received an inexpensive starter guitar for my 14th birthday, along with lessons from a fellow named Denny Zager. Denny had made it to the top of the music world in 1969 as part of the folk-rock duo Zager and Evans by recording the number one song, "In the Year 2525." Denny was (and is) a quiet and humble guy who loved to work on guitars, which may explain why, five years after having a number one hit, he was teaching guitar lessons to kids like me in Lincoln, Nebraska. I remember learning "Puff the Magic Dragon" and "Freight Train," using the Merle Travis finger-picking style. Those lessons lasted about nine months, and then I stopped going because I wasn't practicing enough to make it worth Denny's time. Throughout high school, I played off and on with friends, but I never had the opportunity or occasion to play music in any class other than band, and certainly not in English class, where our attention was focused on Homer, Dickens, and the dictionary. Honestly, I don't even remember my high school English classes, although I remember my English teachers as competent and nice people.

During the summer of 1979, having one year of college under my belt, I took a job working in the Great North Woods of Minnesota as a counselor at a canoeing camp, and because I took my guitar with me, I was expected to play. That's when I first started writing songs. I didn't take it very seriously, as I was naively ambitious to write the next great American novel, or at least to write articles for National Geographic. Playing and writing songs was for fun and for hanging out with friends, not for learning. However, a couple of years later, during an undergraduate survey of 18th Century British Literature at UC-Santa Barbara, our professor required his class to develop dramatic interpretations of William Congreve's, *The Way of The World* and perform them for the class in the professor's back yard. Hoping to contribute something of value to my group's interpretation, I set one of the songs in the play to music for our performance. That assignment was one of only two or three assignments in my undergraduate experience that required or even allowed for artistic license. Playing that song now, nearly 40 years later, takes me right back to that professor's back yard and to that time in my life, creating a vivid memory.

Joshua:

I hate to start with a cliché, but music has always been a part of my life. My parents grew up during hip-hop's conception in the late '70s. They often recount stories of me as a baby, strapped in the car seat, rapping song lyrics word for word—one of my anthems being "Jump" by duo Kris Kross. To this day, I can remember that song's video vividly: Kris Kross wore their jackets backward and baggy, with fresh linings and slits in the eyebrows. After the first time I saw that video, I was hooked on the rhythm, the style, the art, and young Black kids having fun and living life. I wanted to embody that same joy.

My parents loved music. My mom was a member of a breakdancing crew called the "Tidal Waves." Breakdancing, articulated by the "B-girls" and "B-boys," is one of the five pillars of Hip Hop, alongside the DJ, Emcee, Graffiti artists, and the spreading of Knowledge. 2Pac was my parents' favorite artist, and when he died, they took it so hard that you would have thought one of their close relatives had passed. My mother had "sounds" (i.e., stereo sound system) in her Isuzu, which were two 15-inch subwoofers that pumped bass so loudly that it caused surrounding car alarms to activate, and you could hear the trunk-rattling and literally feel the bass in your soul. Too Short, 8Ball & MJG, Crucial Conflict, Do Or Die, Erykah Badu, were a few of the artists that would get "play" in the truck via compact disc. My father would always tell me that he and his cousins were part of a rap group called NOTR, which stood for "N-words Over Thirty Rapping." I never heard a single song from them, but they repped the crew nonetheless and would always tell me that I would too become a member when I turned thirty. Now that I have reached thirty, I am still waiting for my invitation.

I am also influenced by the many family members that are DJ's; my grandfather to this day blasts "the oldies" and, to my surprise, is up to date on some of the contemporary tunes. My grandmothers sing for the church, humming spirituals as they season greens and bake mac and cheese on Sunday mornings. My partner and I love to have music playing in our home at any time of the day while we talk, work, relax, hang out, cook, and clean. There are few moments in our home when music is not being played. Music is essentially life for me and can be considered a sort of saving grace.

Having grown up immersed in music, creating music was the natural progression. I started making music in middle school. I used to sit in the cafeteria before class writing remixes to my favorite songs. One of my favorite remixes I made was of Nelly and The St. Lunatics' "Air Force 1's." If you know, you know that Air Force Ones, aka Forces, aka G-Fazos, aka 1s, were the hottest shoes on the street. I stayed with a pair of white 1's growing up, no creases, forever crispy, no kream.

Later, I graduated from writing songs in the cafeteria to writing and recording songs over free beats I found on the internet. I started devoting a substantial amount of my time to working on my craft. I wrote more songs in high school than I wrote papers but those songs were not for class. I pulled all-nighters writing and recording music on my laptop microphone but could hardly find the motivation to put forth even an ounce of that effort towards school work. But the reality is, I couldn't devote that time to writing school-assigned essays because those assignments felt so distant from my experience. Music, such an integral part of my existence, was given no space in my school's English curriculum.

Tim:

During my first year teaching high school English in Sonora, California, my senior English Literature students were stumbling out of the gates with *Beowulf*, and I found myself sitting at home wondering what to do to liven things up a bit. Over the following day or two, I composed "The Ballad of Beowulf," which was an irreverent take on the Anglo-Saxon epic that included a few jokes but otherwise stayed faithful to the text. The students seemed to like it, but perhaps they were just being polite. I tried my hand at setting some Medieval ballads to music, and also some of Shakespeare's sonnets. My class became a space where students might be sung to or read to, depending on the day. It did not occur to me at the time that the real magic lay in the possibility of my students writing songs based on what we were reading in class, although the evidence for those possibilities surrounded me in the other artistic efforts my students made. One student, unprompted by me, created a painting that visualized characters in different situations described in the literature we had read, perhaps just to ease her boredom. Impressed with her work, I put it on one of the classroom walls, and soon, other students asked if they could bring artwork that they had done and display it on the same wall. Thus, my classroom became a de facto art gallery, as our school apparently had no other place for students to display their work.

And the evidence of what artistic efforts students could achieve was not limited to visual art. As a culminating project for our *Othello* unit, students performed scenes to communicate their interpretations of the text, and they insisted that we reserve the auditorium for the performances. They brought in a variety of costumes and props, again, unprompted, and made Shakespeare's tragedy into their own tragicomic story. In retrospect, I realize that those students taught me their need to open creative spaces in English class.

During the spring of that first year, a fellow English teacher, John Dossi, the music teacher, Pat Sieben, and I formed a teacher-student rock band with seven or eight of the school's best musicians. We performed for school assemblies and at civic events over the following three years, combining rock and roll standards with original songs written by John and by me. Students contributed material that interested them and original solos as part of the ensemble. Playing music along with those students taught me that they had all the tools they needed to generate original music in the classroom. It also taught me that my own songwriting was an important part of my work in the world, and I have continued to write and perform music over the past four decades.

Joshua:

My art integration methods are greatly influenced by colleagues and professors, and surprisingly not so much influenced by my secondary schooling experience as a student. During my first-year teaching at a Chicago nonprofit, High Jump Chicago, one of my mentors, Cory Stevenson, took me under his wing and introduced me to creative ways of engaging students socio-emotionally through art integration. Cory, an artist by trade, offers plenty of opportunities for his students to express themselves artistically, integrating audio/visual elements into High Jump's humanities course. The High Jump campus directors were also very supportive of any and all creative integration and continuously partnered with teachers in allocating the necessary resources needed, whether it be art supplies, text, parental support, or support of the school community.

I didn't realize hip hop and my brand of creativity had a place in "mainstream" education until late in my college studies. One of my undergrad professors, Dr. Timothy Scherman, didn't really speak past the first few class sessions; instead, class time was student-led. Having more autonomy in the classroom allowed me the opportunity to integrate music into my class projects for the 19th Century Women's Literature course. Some professors used other culturally relevant content to teach the curriculum. For example, Professor Sunni Ali used a Boondocks comic strip about white-washed history coupled with some song lyrics by Public Enemy about the shortcomings of education from their eyes. I was a student in a Hip Hop Composition course taught by Dr. Christopher Castillo. In that course, the students were split up into groups of three. In those groups we produced a beat, wrote a song, shot a music video, all in collaboration with one another. At the end of the term, we had a viewing session and we all got to see and hear what the other groups were working on. The best thing about that course was not the music, though that was great; it was that I learned alongside and built meaningful relationships with classmates whom I may never have talked to on the day to day. There were people who did not even really listen to or know much about Hip Hop partaking in the artform. I learned about them through their writing and they learned about me as well.

Dr. Emily Garcia, the instructor for my Caribbean literature course, hosted an open mic/art walk for our final project and extended the invitation to the Northeastern Illinois University (NEIU) community. Each student had space to showcase their projects. Although most students chose a creative medium, some students decided to write an essay, and those students still participated by giving the audience the rundown of their critical analysis via slideshow presentation or other medium. For my final project, I chose to create a song based on the diaries of Maria Teresa "Mate" Mirabal from Julia Alvarez's *In the Time of the Butterflies*. The book is about four sisters and their roles as part of a revolution against Dominican dictator, Rafael Trujillo. To create the song's beat and stay true to the hip hop art form, I started "digging" for samples online searching for "Caribbean songs about revolution." I am not a fluent Spanish speaker, but Google Translate helped me translate the works from Spanish to English. After some time listening to potential samples, I came across "Fuego En El 23!" by Sonora Poncena. Next, it was time for me to "chop" the sample or, in other words, cut parts I wanted to use for the beat and rearrange them how I saw fit to sort of recycle the original song and make it into something new. When writing the song, I had to constantly reference back to important moments in the book because the music is based on Mate's diaries, which I reimagined into a rhyme book for the sake of the project. Accompanying the song, I had to create an artist statement as a way to analyze parts of the story and to explain the moves I made for the song and how the book influenced the project. The assignment was meaningful and creative. It involved some prose, and more importantly, built genuine instructor-to-students, students-to-students, and students-to-audience connections, not to mention maduros and rice from Jamaican and Puerto Rican restaurants *chefs kiss.

Out of my many educational experiences, I remember those moments of cultural integration the most; they had a large impact on my education, likely because they were engaging and fun, but also because they gave me the opportunity to creatively connect with class content. I am fortunate and privileged to say that I have had professors that either built art into the curriculum or were open to me requesting to submit something creative outside of traditional prose.

Tim:

Another awakening in my artistic sensibilities happened in the late 1980s, during an attempt to reconnect to my original dream of writing fiction through a master's program at the University of Nebraska. I enrolled in an elective class called "Adult Painting." The instructor for that class, Brad Krieger, taught me an approach to art and life that has influenced me for decades. Krieger understood the paralyzing lack of confidence that many people experience when faced with the task of being creative, especially when it comes to painting. He told me, "Some people are so afraid of making a mistake, that they will freeze while facing an empty canvas. I just want to give them a big brush dipped in paint and say, 'Swipe it across the canvas. It'll change your life.'" Krieger helped me to understand that the worst thing that can happen when creating a painting is that you create a bad one, in which case you just set it aside and start another. The same can be said for any work of art produced by amateurs or professionals. The freedom to make mistakes is essential to the creative process and, I would argue, the interpretive process as well. Why should our first draft reading be completely accurate? How do we develop an interpretation after we have started it? The arts provide ways of addressing the problem of interpretation that traditional modes of inquiry, such as discussion and essay writing, may not access.

During my doctoral studies, I had the time and opportunity to trace the development of music, visual arts, and performing arts integration into core disciplines as a teaching practice. The use of music and lyrics to learn non-musical subjects is a tradition that goes back to ancient times, and the effects of music integration into other school disciplines has been studied for decades, though the practice of music integration in all subjects, including ELA, remains sparse. When Brock Dethier published his book, *From Dylan to Donne: Bridging English and Music* (2003), he invited practitioners to bring songs into their literary studies to build reading skills and, in one sense, to demystify the classics. My research revealed that teachers are hesitant to incorporate music or other art forms mainly because of their lack of self-confidence as artists (Smardo, 1984; Allen, 1996). While the Music Educators' National Conference (MENC) advocated for music integration into core subjects dating back to the 1960's (Ernst & Gary, 1965), the practice has faced persistent obstacles, including lack of resources for bringing the arts into ELA classrooms, lack of collaboration between English teachers and music specialists, and the pressures of standardized testing. What I found in my own study is that, while over 90% of English teacher respondents (n=245) claimed that they incorporate music into their teaching, their efforts were typically limited to activities that cast students as listeners (consumers) rather than creators (Duggan, 2003). Occasionally, teachers paired music with literature from their curriculum, and less frequently, they used music to relax students. My main takeaway from that study was that students very seldomly engage in the creative process of making music and writing lyrics in English class. Remembering what my students had done back at Sonora High helped me to recognize the need to open those creative spaces as a fully integrated component of English class.

Around 1999, I became involved with the South Dakota Governor's Camp, a residential summer program focusing on academic, artistic, and leadership enrichment for students aged 12–18. Seeing how middle and high school students, freed from the constraints of impending grades and traditional school assignments, grew in their confidence and general intellectual curiosity led me to establish a scholarship contest for them (Duggan,

2007). The contest required applicants to take a concept that they had learned during the past year in school and represent that concept through artistic means. Contest winners included a series of abstract paintings to represent the Battle of Lexington and Concord, an illustrated brochure to represent intracellular organisms, and an iambic pentameter poem to represent an element on the periodic table—further evidence that artistic responses to learning in all disciplines can lead to expanded perspective and understanding of those concepts.

When I entered the field of teacher education, I dedicated much of my research/creative activity to developing workshops to integrate the arts into content area classrooms, focusing primarily, but not exclusively, on English language arts classes. Having a background in the use of performance techniques to teach Shakespeare's texts, and having learned over the span of two decades how using music and other art forms to access literary texts allowed students to create their own unique interpretations of the literature, I began infusing my teaching methods courses with workshop activities that required my preservice teachers to generate assignments that included artistic responses to literature (and life). Having those opportunities built my preservice teachers' sense of their own voice and gave them confidence to include arts integration into their own teaching. However, my less musically inclined students remained doubtful about their own ability to incorporate music, art, and movement into their teaching because they felt that they did not have the tools to do so.

In response to the reticence that many of my students have felt toward arts integration as a function of their own lack of confidence as artists/musicians, and remembering what I had learned from Brad Krieger about overcoming the common fear of artistic failure, I developed the M.A.S.T.E.R. framework for integrating student musical composition and performance (Duggan, 2016; See Appendix B). The acronym refers to Mnemonics, Adaptation, Setting, Theme, Extension/Exploration, and Recital. These avenues for musical interpretation of texts allow students (and teachers) who have little or no musical background to create simple musical responses to literature as a way to express their interpretations of the texts. I have conducted these workshops in local, state, and national forums, including the NCTE Annual Convention, the annual conference of the Children's Music Network, and the National Association for Gifted Children. These workshops have been an ongoing component of my work with pre-service teachers. I also consciously include opportunities for them to draw, paint, or sculpt their interpretations of various aspects of literature. Thankfully, with the publication of *A Symphony of Possibilities* (Zoss & Macro, 2019) and other texts such as this one, teacher educators have a number of tools to choose from to involve their students in artistic production and consumption as a pillar of their encounters with literary texts and their thinking about effective teaching.

Joshua:

Music engulfs us, it's on our radios, "internets," and in nature. But, notably, the core curriculum lacks music. I want to bring more music into the classroom because it is a great tool to engage students, harness their talents, and overall make the classroom more lively and fun. Students come into the classroom all the time singing songs, dancing, and wearing headphones. It seems like such a simple engagement tool to just ask a student what they are listening to and then find some way to incorporate it into the course material. Music is language, so why not include it in our English Language Arts curriculum?

That "why not" is exactly why during my pre-student-teaching clinical experience, I integrated contemporary music lyrics alongside Shakespeare, Langston Hughes, and Maya Angelou for our poetry unit. I had no direct interaction with the students due to Covid, but I was able to pre-record video lessons and upload them onto YouTube, and then my cooperating teacher (CT) would play them for the students. My clinical CT, Ms. Crystal Lennix, shared with me that students thought it was cool to examine the literary devices of Lil' Baby on top of canonical selections. That authentic gesture goes a long way in terms of connecting with students because, too often, much of what they enjoy is ignored and shunned out of the academic space for more traditional content.

My partner in this collaborative project, Tim, sings songs in class while playing his guitar as a typical classroom activity. One assignment that I thought was cool is when we, as a class, wrote a song together. This activity took place in the heart of online learning in a virtual environment that made it increasingly difficult to connect with your peers and instructors. Tim provided a guitar loop and a chorus that he wrote, and we as a class were to fill in the verses with our thoughts. If some of us weren't comfortable expressing ourselves to the melody, there was a segment to just simply use our voices however we pleased; we could do something as manageable as talk alongside the beat without worrying about catching the rhythm. Of course, some of my classmates were nervous for various reasons, including doing something outside of the norm. The activity was fun nonetheless and afforded me another way to think about integrating music into the classroom.

Tim:

Getting to know who our pre-service teachers are as people is vital to providing effective mentorship to them as they pursue their goals of entering our profession. In the first class in the sequence of two discipline-specific English methods courses in our teacher preparation program, I typically assign a writing portfolio based on the National Writing Project's core tenet of practice that English teachers should develop their own identities as writers. Included in the options for students to explore for their portfolios is to write, produce, and perform music. While in that class, Joshua shared a couple of his musical compositions as part of his portfolio, and he indicated an interest in music integration as a fundamental part of his teaching ELA. It became clear early on that Joshua was serious about his music and about making it a vital component of his teaching. During the second course in the sequence, students and I composed a song together along the theme of "Be good at what you do," and we read *Critical Media Pedagogy* by Ernest Morrell, Rudy Dueñas, Veronica Garcia, and Jorge López (2013), a book which foregrounds the necessity of involving students in critical media production, rather than simply casting them in the role of critical media consumers. It was no surprise to me when Joshua entered his student teaching that he would engage his students in music and other artistic production.

Joshua:

During my student-teaching field experience, my CT, Ms. Elena Perez, and I were brainstorming ways to incorporate something creative for the student's final project for our unit on *Night* by Elie Wiesel. It was somewhat of a challenge because we had to assess students on particular cognitive skills, one being counterclaims. After days of throwing around ideas and abandoning many of them, we thought that it would be cool for the students to counter my argument for the most prevalent theme in the story. I wanted to assign something with an artistic element because art can be a cultivated skill that can lead to creative interpretations of texts using images, emotions, and imagination to represent themes, characters, ideas, and so on (Hartman, et al., 2019). Thinking of a way to incorporate that artistic element, I thought, hey, I can write and record a song related to a theme in the story and have the students counter that with a creative piece that represents a theme of their choosing. Ms. Perez gave me the green light, and I was off to create the instructional handout and the lyrics for the song. The theme I selected for my argument as most prevalent in *Night* was "the relationship between father and son." When thinking about the story and who it was centered around, I noticed that Elie's father, although a major character in the story, never really gets to tell his story. He has no voice. I used that idea to craft lyrics for a song I titled, "Night From My Eyes." (https://bit.ly/3V2X8FZ) I wrote the song from the perspective of Elie's father as a response to his son's story and the trauma experienced by both of them. After crafting the lyrics, it was time to record. I usually produce but found myself in a bit of a time crunch, so I searched online for some free beats to write and record to in order to save some time. After recording the song, mixing and mastering, came the time for the students to hear it.

The song serves two purposes, one being to connect a piece of art to a theme, and two being to provide an avenue for the students to counter my chosen theme with their own choice and artistic representation of what they considered the most prevalent theme in the text. When I premiered the song for students, the Google Hangouts chat went UP! I previously told students that I made music as a hobby, but judging by the responses, they didn't expect my music to be good (I still don't know how to take that). From that moment, it seemed as though the students were fired up and ready to create. Using a net monitoring system, I could see some students composing music of their own, some drawing, some writing poetry, doing whatever it is they like to do creatively. It was a big part of the project design to give students a choice in their selected theme and the creative medium. Allowing choice can be used as a way to "humanize" and democratize the classroom in the sense of working together to produce and analyze class content (Rhym, 2016). Oftentimes, students are told what to do at every step and this can leave them feeling as though their thoughts and skills don't matter as much as what the teacher wants them to do.

When it was time for students to turn in their projects, I created Google Slide presentations for each class and a folder for all of the classes so the students could showcase their work for their peers and do a virtual gallery walk to view, read, watch, and listen to what their classmates created. Below are some examples of student work with our commentary.

(https://bit.ly/3I50Vup)

For instance, Jonathan countered my theme with a song of his own titled "Fighting for Survival," using the theme survival. In the song, Jonathan chronicles how Elie and the Jews had to rely on each other in order to survive the horrors of the Holocaust. The theme of survival was the most prevalent theme to Jonathan because that was the most crucial thing on Elie's mind throughout the story. Jonathan writes about how Elie and his father "used each other if they ever needed a revival" while walking in the snow where the focus was just on staying alive. Jonathan's song shows his understanding of this major theme of survival, seeing the Nazis "stealing [their] spirits right out of [their] souls." The song also demonstrates his willingness to engage and produce meaningful work that you can bop to.

Vero created a visual representation using the theme of dehumanization tied to one of the most memorable scenes in the text by way of a comic strip using the line "The stomach alone was measuring time" (Wiesel, 52; See Figure 8.1). Looking at Vero's artwork, one can tell the very detailed approach to the art form. The lower right panel represents a display of

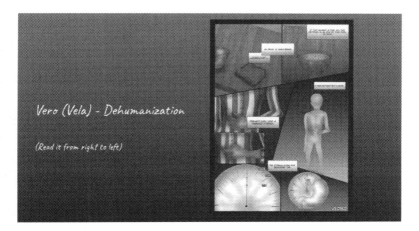

Figure 8.1

a stomach superimposed on a clock. Our minds keep time and that time could seemingly pass faster or slower depending on elemental needs, like food. Elie's stomach measuring the time takes the responsibility from the mind and puts it on the body because as Elie says at the time, "[he] was nothing but a body" (Wiesel, 52). Taking words and making them visual is an interpretive skill and implies a basic literacy question: "When you read something, what is going through your mind?" Art allows us to visually articulate what our minds "see" and share our ideas and talents with others.

Feelings That Didn't Fade Away

For things you don't do, you feel regret.
You feel a blackhole in your heart that never seems to go away.
And overtime that blackhole only seems to grow bigger and bigger.
Because sometimes time doesn't heal everything you want it to heal.
Every little thing starts reminding you of what you could've done
to not stand where you stand now.
You try to find solace but all you get left with is despair.
The only hope you feel
is that one day you'll be able to go back
and fix everything you messed up
and change your thoughts.
Father, I'm sorry I thought of letting you go.
I'm sorry for not wanting to hold your hand
when you needed me the most.
And I'm sorry I did not want to listen to you
when you needed me to hear you out.

But the thought of you being alone in the dark was enough for me
   to stay.
To keep you safe.
So, blame me for what I'm unforgivable for.
But know that you and I have fought our battles together.
No matter where you are now,
I will continue to fight.
For a better life, father.

—Diya

Throughout history, poetry has been used as a tool of healing, resistance, and reflection (Baxley & Sealey-Ruiz, 2021). Diya taps into that long history with her poem "Feelings That Didn't Fade Away." Using the theme of guilt/inaction, Diya reflects from the perspective of Elie wishing he could have done something to save his father's life. Diya's work transcends the text because the words in this poem can be applied to one's own life and feelings of guilt. As I read Diya's poem, I catch myself thinking about the family and friends that have passed at an early age and questioning whether or not I could have done anything to influence the situation or even why I am still here in my 30s when so many are taken from us before they reach their mid-20s. Diya's poem makes me think about survivor's guilt and having to live with the unanswered questions that come with it.

Selene produced a cartoon-like visual representation using the theme of dehumanization (Figure 8.2). In this piece, we see many sets of eyes gazing at a hot cauldron of soup as if it were prey. Disembodying the eyes of Elie and the other prisoners dehumanizes them while, ironically, emphasizing their very

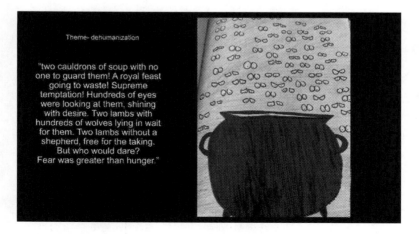

Figure 8.2

human mixed emotions. Some of the eyes display anger, some fear, and some anxiety, but all of them long for sustenance. The very size of the cauldron of soup emphasizes the prisoners' desire to eat, and their animal-like smallness. Those eyes and the very humans they represent, however, are aware that eating would come with a death sentence, and, in Wiesel's words, the "fear was greater than hunger" (59). Selene's work shows how dehumanization and fear work in tandem, forcing the oppressed to self-police and deny themselves basic-human necessities such as food to nourish their own bodies.

(https://bit.ly/42Ll2rd)

D'jeniah recorded an acoustic singer-songwriter tune titled "Generational Trauma" using the theme of dehumanization and inspired by Wiesel's Nobel Prize acceptance speech. D'jeniah is a talented writer, but the recording adds another element to the words on the page. You can hear the somber angst in her tone, in the rhythm that is soothing, and the softening ukulele. Her repetition of the last two lines, "There's so much to get done. / I hope they get it done," both emphasizes and calls into question the hopefulness of Wiesel's acceptance speech. As D'jeniah sings, Elie was undoubtedly part of a "traumatized generation," a generation that lived through genocide. D'jeniah's song is presented in a way that codes Elie's sadness in a pleasant melody and the sweet tones from the ukulele.

In her illustration, Ariadna conveys her interpretation of the theme of guilt/inaction, using the color blue to resemble a sort of crippling guilt that can limit one's ability to move (Figure 8.3). Ariadna also includes a shadowy figure on the wall that represents the horrors that are "happening in front

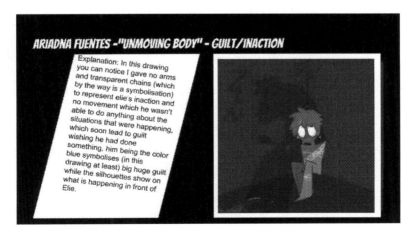

Figure 8.3

of Elie." The figure is also bound in transparent chains: intangible, but still real, like survivor's guilt. The piece as a whole symbolizes the internalization of survivor's guilt and how what is on the outside may not illustrate the full picture. We don't know what someone has truly been through. Ariadna's art makes me think about the importance of giving grace to others as well as oneself.

The ELA classroom and any classroom for that matter can and should be a place where students can harness their talents and use them as a vehicle to connect with class material. Arts integration serves our students in a more holistic way by leveraging their interests, voices, and skills to enter the conversation and to democratize the classroom. As a teacher and lifelong student, I find that I best learn in enjoyable spaces, spaces that value me, and spaces that challenge and allow me to show up as who I am. With that being said, the arts are a big part of who we are as people, so why not make it an essential part of the classroom experience? Of course, like anything else, it will take practice and patience to find what works for you and the humans in front of you, but along the journey there will be many opportunities for you and your students to connect to one another, build relationships, and develop talents in a genuine democratic way. I am still working on finding ways to relinquish more authority in the classroom to foster a collaborative learning environment and a less authoritative one.

Tim:

What I found compelling about the project that Joshua and Ms. Perez put together is how they tied the artistic elements with the cognitive skills in a way that opens up lateral thinking for the students. Can we think of making claims and counterclaims as a musical or visual dialogue between characters in a text? When students write formulaic five-paragraph essays that include a "counter-argument" as a gesture to potential opposing viewpoints, they are often encouraged to take a fill-in-the-form approach to structure and sequence. What students sometimes do not understand is the connection between such an assignment and the idea of people in the real world earnestly debating different perspectives on real issues that affect their lives. By introducing the *Night* project with his own musical piece constructed from the perspective of the father, Joshua set up a situation wherein he could say to his students, now it's your turn, but I've already chosen the father's perspective, so you need to choose a different character or different perspective on the story as a counter to mine.

This notion of building an artistic dialogue around a topic is reminiscent of what happened with Christopher Marlowe's poem, "A Passionate Shepherd to His Love," which inspired a number of poetic responses from other poets of the day, including Walter Raleigh and John Donne, as well as later poets, such as Dorothy Parker and William Carlos Williams. Similarly, composers and artists over the centuries have been inspired by literature to create derivative works, and likewise authors have been inspired by artists and musicians to create fiction and poetry. Having students construct art pieces to create a dialogue around a written text they have studied in class is at the heart of our definition of "language arts." Contextualizing the process within an instructional unit that explores one of the worst historical atrocities against humanity allows students to share their growing awareness of the world they inherit and how we have come to our present point in history and culture.

CONCLUSION

During a short interview that Joshua conducted with his cooperating teacher, Elena Perez (see Appendix A), she mentioned that, through the creative project connected with *Night*, her students were "seeing each other...almost for the first time this year." We can't emphasize enough how important it is for students to "see" each other as thinking, feeling, creative people who have something to say, something to contribute, to the larger conversations around them. In an age of profound anxiety produced by serious social, political, cultural, and personal pain, an age that produces existential questions ranging from whether we can continue to grow and thrive as citizens in a democracy to whether we can survive as a species, the arts are not just an escape into "fun," although practicing the arts can be fun. The arts create space to have serious conversations about who we are, who we want to be, and how we can address these pervasive problems that we face.

No doubt we cannot and should not remove essay writing from an English Language Arts course, but English Language Arts can be taught and learned through other works, too. Educators teaching English Language Arts, a course that explores communication and storytelling, may be doing their students a disservice by not tapping into the various modes of communicating and storytelling that students engage in outside of the classroom. Arts integration widens the field of interpreting literature (White, 2019). Students can draw visual interpretations of important scenes, they can write journal entries from the perspective of a character in the story, they can partner with classmates in creating a modern adaptation of a crucial moment in the story, they can write spin-offs—the possibilities are as endless as the boundaries set or the resources at our disposal. Arts integration into the ELA curriculum has the ability to transform how we think about literature and allow students to produce meaningful work that can transcend the classroom (Duggan, 2016). When students create, they produce knowledge

(Zoss & Macro, 2019) that can be on display in the classroom, in the hallways, in books like this, and beyond. Teachers who consciously open space for arts integration give students other avenues to enter the conversation around interpretation, meaning, and significance.

In his essay, "The Heart of a Teacher," educator-activist Parker Palmer (1998) claimed that "we teach who we are." He reasoned that our students know when we are not being true to our identities in our work with them, and that we must not conceal our own sense of pain and joy as we experience them. In reflecting upon our own individual journeys that have led both of us to this place of arts advocacy in the teaching and learning of English, we believe that artistic development is anything but an ancillary benefit or a pleasant side-trip on our road to intellectual and cultural enlightenment. It is, rather, one road we must travel with our students if we wish to reach a more peaceful, more equitable, and more sustainable future.

APPENDIX A
Interview With Elena Perez, Joshua's Cooperating Teacher

Joshua Smith: Okay, here we go. Do you remember the process for us creating the *Night* summative assessment assignment?

Ms. Perez: I think it was really about backwards planning, right? So, like, taking a look at the text and thinking of what we want the kids to gain out of it by the end. And number one, obviously, is always that writing component. For us as English teachers, it's really about having them be not only good readers, but really great writers. And so we always have that essay component and then try to think of a way to also really have something for those kids who aren't great writers, where they can kind of shine with this unit, with this project. And so, I think that's what I was really thinking about in the backwards planning: what do we want to get? And then considering all the kids, you know, we're not just saying, everyone's gonna get an essay, and everyone has to do the same thing, but also saying, okay, everyone is not an artist, or everyone's not a writer, everyone is not an actress, or whatever it may be, and being able to really hone in on those different skills. And I think that project really did that for a lot of those kiddos.

Joshua Smith: So, for the project, I know, we had to align it to the cognitive skills that we were working on throughout the unit. And one was counterclaims, so we had to write counterclaim paragraphs. But we were brainstorming to try to figure out a creative route to take, and I remember that being kind of difficult.

Ms. Perez: Yeah. And I think part of that, too, was because of the remote learning. I think we were trying to consider how the students were currently dealing with remote learning and why we don't even see their faces, or why only half of them are talking to us, like how do we get these other kids to have another outlet because of remote learning?

Joshua Smith: So, do you feel like the lesson had any shortcomings?

Ms. Perez: I think really, it's just about remote learning. I think part of the fun is to have the kids be together as a community, and they can see each other and ask, what are you doing? Oh, you're doing that, you're so cool. That's what we were missing, but I think we got a little bit once you had them display their work in the slideshow, when you had them write in comments. Reading those comments, I wanted to cry. It was like, yes, you guys are seeing each other, I think, almost for the first time this year. And so that was really nice.

Joshua Smith: Yeah, I can definitely see how that will make just everything that much sweeter. So what do you think are some of the strengths of the project?

Ms. Perez: I think just being open to letting the kids do whatever they want. Like, here's a little bit of guidance, but you do with it what you will, you know. You can draw, write poetry, all of these different outlets, and I think they all went in different directions. I think that was a strength of just kind of being able to guide them just a little bit and then just say, go for it and then trust that we were going to be okay with whatever they decided to do. But that was kind of unique to have kids really be like, all right, I'm actually doing it. So that's pretty cool.

Joshua Smith: When you first heard the song that I made, what was your reaction? And then, how did the students react?

Ms. Perez: Number one, I thought, there's no way that that's actually him. And I thought, immediately, it was just really interesting to see you put yourself out there. I love music, but I'm not musically inclined. So, like other projects I've done, I was wanting to have a sample, right. But I noticed I usually use student samples from the previous year. I think the kids really liked that the sample was from you. Like, Oh, my God, he actually did something for us to look at, you know, or listen to. And I think that had more buy-in than just seeing some of the samples from last year, versus like, no, I put some time into this, so you better put some time into this too. And I think they appreciate that for sure. They were in awe and in shock of it for sure. 1,000,000%.

Joshua Smith: Yeah, it was fun. It's definitely a vulnerable thing. Because it's like, oh, what are they gonna say?

Ms. Perez: Yeah, you know, you became a celebrity.

Joshua Smith: Overnight. Yeah. Do you use music in the classroom often? Or is that something that you see a lot in the ELA discipline?

Ms. Perez: Um, I don't see it almost ever, like it's super, super rare. I usually do it when it's quiet time, like if they have to do self-reflections or independent writing or SDL. I would have a sign-up of kids that would do the songs and stuff. Even if it's just like background noise, somehow, it creates this vibe, I can't even explain it. And so being able to give them the outlet to do music for part of their creative project was really nice because, I think for this generation in particular, even through the years, music has just become such a huge outlet for so many of these kids. So, it's kind of nice to see it in the school.

Joshua Smith: Yeah, yeah, I definitely agree. Because music does kind of set a tone and vibe. And I feel like, especially in my ELA, just even looking at song lyrics, that's something that I want to try to do in the future. What do you think, if anything, that my students learned from this project?

Ms. Perez: I think something I maybe just realized it this week because I'm having now some kids who never did that project who are now saying like, can I still do that, I'm like, yeah, go for it. And they're saying, what do I have to do? Or how do I do this? And my directions are very minimal. And what I'm realizing is, I think they're understanding that we respect them. You know, because I feel like a lot of the times when we're asking them to write essays and show comprehension and discussion, I feel for them, it's a lot of expectation, expectation, expectation. And I think when it comes to this creative project, they're so used to the expectations, that for the first time, they're kind of like, wait, I can do whatever? And I'm like, yeah. And so, for the first time, they're seeing teachers as not all about expectations and throwing stuff at them, but thinking,

	they also want to just see who we are as people, you know, and I think they recognize that. I feel like a lot of the kids that we don't normally see, we saw them for the first time through that project.
Joshua Smith:	Yeah. Yeah. I agree with that. Is there anything else that you learned from this project?
Ms. Perez:	I think to do more of it. Because what I'm realizing is, obviously, we do it at the very end of the unit kind of like as an assessment, but how do we do that more frequently throughout a unit, you know? Today, we're going to talk about art from Africa. I know, I'm not an art teacher, but let's do this anyway. And being able to bring more of that into the regular class.

APPENDIX B
M.A.S.T.E.R. Framework

M = Mnemonics. Using musical mnemonics to remember lists of words or concepts has been a staple of early instruction for centuries, including the Alphabet Song and "Uno, Dos, Tres" from *Sesame Street*. When you ask students to remember lists of names, important details, language conventions, or other basic concepts, have them construct their own musical mnemonic devices, using tunes that are familiar to them or original melodies.

A = Adaptations. Great stories have been adapted to song by opera composers and popular musicians, and your students can do their own musical adaptations of the stories they read if you give them the opportunity. You may need to teach basic song structure, such as 1–4–5 progressions in folk or blues, or use your musically inclined students to lead groups in developing melody, but the key is in the verses they compose to retell the story (or event) and the mood that the music helps to create. Students can tie musical elements to story elements, such as having a bridge or a key change at the turning point in the story. Their adaptations may be faithful to the themes and spirit of the original text (as interpreted by the students). Have them write explanations of their composing process and choices.

S = Settings. Setting poetry and story to music is one of the easiest and most rewarding ways to incorporate music into the English classroom. Unlike the adaptation activity, when we do a musical setting, we don't change the words of the poem or story. Ask students to use whatever musical skills they have to take the printed text and set it to music. The focus of this activity is primarily on the musical elements that are used to illuminate the text. Sonnets or other short poems work well.

T = Themes. Does anyone remember "Peter and The Wolf"? Students who play (or who would like to play) musical instruments can compose mono- or multi-tonal themes for individual characters in stories, or to represent different events or actions. The same may be done as "background music" for reading of poems. Have students develop these themes using their own musical instruments or using readily available music software, such as GarageBand or Mini-Moog. Students can then write "artist statements" explaining why they made the various musical choices they made, and how those choices reflect their understanding of the original text. Reader's Theater readings with the theme music can be very powerful.

E = Extensions/Explorations. Imagine a character in a story at a critical moment. In a musical, typically those moments are turned to songs that step outside of the storytelling to illuminate inner conflict or desire (e.g., "Somewhere over the Rainbow"). English teachers often ask students to journal on characters' emotions or to create diary entries from a character's perspective. Why not write a song? Also, students may find a theme or idea in literature that sparks their own thinking, which can lead to original songwriting. Such original songwriting signifies development of independence in the student's literary education.

R = Recital. Remember to give the students the opportunity to perform their compositions. From a recital approach to a festival or competition (if that's what turns you on), sharing the fruits of our musical labor is essential to building community. Follow up with reflective or critical conversations about how music communicates story or emotion and how the creative and analytical mind work together to produce artistic responses to learning.

REFERENCES

Allen, M. A. (1996). The role of music and rhyme in emergent literacy: Teacher perspectives. (Doctoral dissertation, The University of Texas at Austin, 1996). *Dissertation Abstracts International, 57* (06), 2413A.

Baxley, D., & Sealey-Ruiz. (2021). Poetry, healing and resistance. In G. Camparo, A. Stornaiuolo, & E. E. Thomas (Eds.), *Research in the teaching of English* (p. 311). National Council of Teachers of English.

Dethier, B. (2003). *From Dylan to Donne: Bridging English and music.* Heinemann.

Duggan, T. J. (2016). M.A.S.T.E.R.ing the art of music integration. In L. L. Johnson & C. Z. Goering (Eds.), *Recontextualized: A framework for teaching English with music* (pp. 51–64). Sense Publishers.

Duggan, T. J. (2003). *Uses of music in the high school English/language arts classroom in South Dakota: Teacher perceptions and practices.* Unpublished dissertation. University of South Dakota.

Duggan, T. J. (2007). Ways of knowing: Exploring artistic representations of concepts. *Gifted Child Today 30*(4), 56–63.

Ernst, K., & Gary, C. L., eds. (1965). *Music in general education.* Music Educators National Conference, Committee on Music in General Education.

Hartman, P. M., Berg, J., & Schuler, B. (2019). Using artistic response strategies meaningfully in the English language arts classroom. In K. J. Macro & M. Zoss (Eds.), *A symphony of possibilities: A handbook for arts integration in secondary English language arts* (pp. 121–138). National Council of Teachers of English.

Morrell, E., Duenas, R. , Garcia-Garza, V., & Lopez, J. (2013). *Critical media pedagogy: Teaching for achievement in city schools.* Teachers College Press.

Palmer, P. J. (2007). The heart of a teacher. In A. C. Ornstein, E. F. Pajak, & S. B. Ornstein (Eds.), *Contemporary issues in curriculum* (4th ed.; pp. 71–81). Pearson.

Rhym, D. (2016). Hip-hop and social change: Critical pedagogy in the classroom. In L. L. Johnson & C. Z. Goering (Eds.), *Recontextualized: A framework for teaching English with music* (pp. 51–64). Sense Publishers.

Smardo, F. A. (1984). Using children's literature as a prelude or finale to music experiences with young children. *The Reading Teacher, 37,* 700–705.

Wiesel, E., & Wiesel, M. (2006). *Night.* Hill and Wang, a division of Farrar, Straus and Giroux.

White, M. A. (2019). Exploring the possibilities and tensions of visual responses to literature. In K. J. Macro & M. Zoss (Eds.), *A symphony of possibilities: A handbook for arts integration in secondary English language arts* (pp. 98–120). National Council of Teachers of English.

Zoss, M., & Macro, J. K. (2019). Radical visions for the future. In K. J. Macro & M. Zoss (Eds.), *A symphony of possibilities: A handbook for arts integration in secondary English language arts* (pp. 176–179). National Council of Teachers of English.

Printed in the United States
by Baker & Taylor Publisher Services